Illustrations by Miguel A. Reyes-Mariano

2nd edition 2024

STRESS IN THE U.S. MILITARY RESERVE
Stress' Impact of Supervisory Styles in U.S. Navy Reservists
Central New York During the Military Fiscal Year 2013-2014

Author's Notes

Miguel A. Reyes-Mariano[1], Political Science Department: Master in Public Administration and Nonprofit Management at the State University of New York at Buffalo State.

This writer has been part of the United States Navy Reserve for over seventeen years; and for such, decided not to take active part in the study to prevent this relationship to be perceived as a conflict of interest.

Correspondence concerning this master's project research should be addressed to Miguel A. Reyes-Mariano, Master in Public Administration – Political Science Department at SUNY Buffalo State, Classrooms A-301. Email: mr45@buffalo.edu

Abstract

Recent studies on stress[2] have paid close attention to the outcomes of global trends like the wars on terrorism. In this convulsed world of the 21st Century, civilians and military are exposed to a myriad of drawbacks, and everyone has to manage to carry out their lives and duties. The resulting work-related stress is present in a significant number of complaints in medical centers and hospitals; public, private or military. Although the United States Ready Reserve has not received much attention in the past, they are getting it now, given its more active interactions on foreign and domestic public policies. Hence, this research has sought to reflect upon the relationship between stress and supervisory styles in the reserve centers. This study reviewed and critiqued relevant empirical literature of the past two decades concerned with stress in the workplace. It also visited some historical publications on supervision and leadership styles affecting performances. In all, the results showed that the organizational culture is more related to stress than the supervisory styles in a naval reserve center. Still, since there is not a similar research-paper to correlate this outcome, additional studies are needed to ensure a better understanding of what should be the appropriate climate in the reserve centers for military reservists.

Keywords: Stress, Occupational Stress, Stress in the workplace, Stress in military personnel, Leadership Styles affecting stress, Supervisory Styles affecting stress.

Table of Contents

Foreword

Chapter I: Introduction
    Preliminary
    Statement of Problem
    Purpose of Study
    Significance of Study
Chapter II: Review of Related Literature
    Opening Comments
    Review and Critique of Literature
    Summary of Literary rev
Chapter III: Methodology
    Design of Study
    Sample Selection
    Data Collection Methods
    Data Analysis
Chapter IV: Conclusion
    Results, Conclusions, Summary
Chapter V: Discussions
    Possible implications of Outcomes
    Limitations of Study
    Future Research

References

Endnotes

Appendix

    A. Site Agreement NOSC Buffalo
    B. Site Agreement NOSC Rochester
    C. Site Agreement NOSC Syracuse
    D. Informed Consent form
    E. Stress' Impact of Supervisory Styles
       Questionnaire (p.1 &p.2)
    F. Required Sample Size by The Research
       Advisor

Charts, Figures, Tables

Charts
01. Gatfield, T. (2005) Supervisory
    Management Styles
02. Stress in a typical work-day
03. Feedback in a typical work day
04. Critical Values of Chi-square Distribution
Tables
05. Critical Values of Chi-square Distribution
Graphic

Figures
01. Reserve components at time of study
02. Professor Lawrence Shulman permission to adapt
    questionnaires from "International Supervision" (3rd Ed)

Tables
Demographics
Age in years: Statistics[3] and percentages
01. Sex: Statistics and percentages
02. Ethnicity: Statistics and percentages
03. Time in service: Statistics and percentages
04. Pay grade -Enlisted: Statistics and percentages
05. Pay grade -Officer: Statistics and percentages
06. Time in grade: Statistics and percentages
07. Education: Statistics and percentages

Questions

08. Q01-Mood changes last year: Statistics and percentages
09. Q02-How often you felt stressed?: Statistics and percentages
10. Q03-How often Supervisor gave feedback in a typical day?: Statistics and percentages
11. Q04-How often you felt harassed by Supervisor last year?: Statistics and percentages
12. Q05-How often you felt bullied by Supervisor last year?: Statistics and percentages
13. Q06- How often you felt discriminated by Supervisor last year?: Statistics and percentages
14. Q07-How satisfied with autonomy Supervisor gave you to do your work?: Statistics and percentages
15. Q08- How satisfy with the work of those reporting to you?: Statistics and percentages
16. Q09-How well are responsibilities shared among team members?: Statistics and percentages
17. Q10-How well know command's mission?: Statistics and percentages
18. Q11-How well know command's structure?: Statistics and percentages
19. Q12-How well know command's operations?: Statistics and percentages
20. Q13-How well communicate with Supervisor?: Statistics and percentages
21. Q14-Being defensive towards Supervisor: Statistics and percentages
22. Q15-Involment of Supervisor in Career Planning: Statistics and percentages
23. Q16-Supervisor explained Command's mission: Statistics and percentages
24. Q17-Supervisor explained Command's structure: Statistics and percentages
25. Q18-Supervisor explained Command's operations: Statistics and percentages
26. Q19-Knowing what is expected from you all the time: Statistics and percentages
27. Q20-Access to necessary resources to do your work: Statistics and percentages

28. Q21-Good working relations with Supervisor: Statistics and percentages
29. Q22-Command contributing to professional development: Statistics and percentages
30. Q23-Stress reducing quality of performances: Statistics and percentages
31. Q24-Use of alcohol to reduce stress: Statistics and percentages
32. Q25-Sleep problems before or after drill days: Statistics and percentages
33. Q26-How easy is to find opportunities to advance in military career?: Statistics and percentages
34. Q27-Example of Supervisor is very inspiring: Statistics and percentages
35. Q28-Is work pace expected from you always reasonable?: Statistics and percentages
36. Q29-Experiences of unexplained anger after leaving workplace: Statistics and percentages
37. Q30-Feeling that there is no other place with you fit in outside military life: Statistics and percentages
38. Q31-Exciment about meaningfulness of military work: Statistics and percentages

Comments
39. Comments: Statistics and percentages

STRESS IN THE U.S. MILITARY RESERVE

Foreword

There are realities not easily palpable to the common senses, which is the reason why scientists and scholars dedicate their time to study diverse phenomena, no matter how insignificant they may seem. On the other hand, there are highly visible problems that seem to have no explanations—period. For example, suicides, that not only raises questions about the condition of the victim but also confronts the community with the intangibles of the implications with the otherness.

In this sense, the blueprint adopted in this research study focused on the effort to explore one entity and a process of public administration, and a problem affecting this entity and this process. The entity was the Naval Operational Support Center in the Department of Navy under the Department of Defense, which reports to the Executive Branch. The process considered was "supervision," with the knowledge that it affects equally supervisees and supervisors. The problem was "stress," understood as a state of physical or mental instability resulting from factors that tend to upset a person's psychic internal balance, and in the worst-case scenario this can lead to suicides.

Unfortunately, in the U.S. Armed forces, suicides attributable to stress have claimed far too many lives. During the wars in Iraq and

Afghanistan, more soldiers committed suicide than were killed by the enemy (Tick, 2014). According to Edward Tick, an expert on post-traumatic stress disorder (PTSD) and the founding director of *"Soldier's Heart: Veterans' Safe Return Programs,"* stress is the silent enemy. Suicides have occurred in such alarming numbers that now we are confronted not only by the moral issue implied. One only needs to calculate the annual cost of a reservist's training to understand the financial burdens. This cost includes not only the loss of a human life but also the loss of the investment in the training of the deceased to which is added the cost of the training of a new soldier.

Now, in regard to how these three elements are related to Public Administration, one needs to reflect upon the following. First, as mentioned, the reserve is part of the Department of the Navy under the Department of Defense, which reports to the head of the Executive Branch (the Commander-in-Chief of the Military). Second, the Navy Reserve in the State of New York makes up the Navy Militia, which report directly to the governor, just like the National Guard. In this sense, this entity helps to frame the political policies when it comes to safeguard the state from foreign or domestic enemies. Third, many reservists are moonlighting in federal, state, and local government public offices. Some of them are even in high-level positions where they are contributing to the definition and implementation of national policies. For example, there are reservists known by the researcher in executive positions in the Transportation Security Administration (TSA), which controls national security throughout all airports across the nation.

In addition, it is well-known that police officers, firefighters, teachers, social service workers, and even agents of special bureaus are supplementing their incomes through their participation in the military reserve. In a way, some of them are contributing to the development or implementation of public policies in crucial institutions with missions tied to the national security of the United States of America.

Chapter I: Introduction

To begin, let's touch on the aesthetics and how practical is this study. This writer needs to acknowledge that this is a research study intended for a broader audience rather than the exclusiveness of few scholars and professionals. There were no efforts in trying to gain any merits from the sophistication of the narrative. In like manner, the statistical analysis was rather practical than perplexing. The writer also tailored to the breadth needed for the study all the arguments taken from preeminent authors from the literary review. Al this does not detract credits from hoisting the voice of the service members who selflessly participated in the study. For such, it is more a case study than a breakthrough in knowledge. Nonetheless, it contributed by eliminating the supervisory styles as independent variable from the equation of the stress in the military reserve center in Central New York.

Preliminaries

The military reserve is an invaluable resource to safeguard the stability of any nation. However, there is nothing more valuable than the good health and well-being of the members of that combatant force. For this reason, it is essential that reservists demonstrate excellent mental and physical health to respond to the challenging duty of serving their country when necessary.

Because the physical training of reservists, as well as their good mental health, is paramount, it is pertinent to provide reservists with appropriate coaching in an effective environment supported by an appropriate supervision (as a process more significant than just directing what a subordinate does)[4](Asgar & Hoffman, 1989, p. 1). It should no be any less, given that national security may depend on it. Moreover, supervisory styles[5] need special consideration too since each organization should not only take into account the unique characteristics of each member, but those of their particular group as a whole too. (Supervisory Styles Chart #1 p. 25-26). Only having members in the military reserve who are physically and mentally ready and sound can ensure their resourcefulness. *De facto*[6], the flexibility and effectiveness of this force are essential to support tactical military operations or missions of national interest at any given time.

In this sense, this research concentrated on determining whether or not stress exists in a reservist's workplace. Extensive studies have shown that this somatic[7] response is responsible for a large number of illnesses that diminish humans' potential abilities, which are essential to military personnel. Therefore, this study was designed to establish whether there was any relationship between supervisory styles and stress in reserve centers in

Central and Western New York during the operational year of 2013-2014.

There are who question the relationship between the Military and the

Public Administration giving that military presence essentially lies outside

the continental United States (OCONUS). In any case, most of the training of

reservists that is the matters in this project has taken place in the continental

United States (CONUS). Traditionally, the military in America had been an

instrument of foreign policy; however, that changed since September 11th,

2001, when the national security was greatly impacted. Since then, the

military participation in domestic public policies has dramatically increased

in projects of all nature, some of which are truly national secrets.

In some countries, such as the United Kingdom, Spain and the

United States of America, members of the military reserves are civilians

(United States. Office of the Chief Army Reserve., p. 14), who maintain

parallel "*labour*[8]" relations in the public or private sector. These reservists

can participate individually, or as members of reserve units assigned to

particular active combatant components of the armed forces. On these

ancillaries'[9] services or their combined roles as civilians and soldiers, these

citizens are required to maintain their military skills through monthly

training.

According to the United States Department of Defense (DOD)[10], after the attack on the World Trade Center on September 11, 2001, and by the end of August 2014, approximately 899,510 reservists had been activated. This represents nearly 60% of all military personnel who were permanently on active duty during that time, roughly 1,500,000. Even after the official end of the war in Iraq, and with the conflict in Afghanistan anticipated to end by December, 2014, there are still 33,426 reservists on active duty, in contrast to the 92,000 activated during 2011 (Figure #1). Nonetheless, these numbers indicate the important role this component of the armed forces plays in safeguarding national security.

For those reservists, continuous training is necessary to keep them up to date with all the changes in the various military roles of their active counterpart ranks[11]. This is essential, in order for them to be able to be activated at any time. This training usually occurs one weekend per month and on programmatic active duties, two weeks a year. In the case of the United States Navy Reserve, the site in which they are trained is called Naval Operational Reserve Center or NOSC (Ramchand & Center for Military Health Policy Research., 2011, p. xxxii).

The NOSC has an active-duty staff, which is composed in the top of their charts by a Commanding Officer (CO), sometimes an Executive Officer

(XO), and a Chief of the Command (the most senior on active duty). There are also Leading Petty Officers (LPOs) for the different administrative components (Administration, Training, Medical, Dental, Logistics, Operations, etc.). Finally, there are sailors who rank from E-1 to E-9, being E-5/E-6 and above considered as Supervisors of lower rank service-members.

The NOSC is responsible for the operation of the reserve center. Each one of the distinctive units that drill there has its own CO, XO, Chief of the Command, LPOs, and their officers and sailors. During this study, there were eight different units in the target NOSC in Syracuse, New York that represent the leadership and supervisory style of the particular Commanders in each of the units.

With regard to the NOSC operations, the training is very different from that of the initial military training at the Recruit Training Command (RTC)[12]. While Boot Camp training prepares soldiers to withstand the most terrible situations, it does not provide any additional benefits to reservists who have already passed such training. Thus, if servicemen or officers need to refresh their survival skills for the battlefield, they are well aware that serious training will be required to survive the squalors[13] and rigors of war.

In fact, the integration of stress is an essential part of this arduous training, as a reasonable amount of it can help a combat soldier when in the battleground.

Nonetheless, the stress that can contribute to the survival on the battlefield can be lethal if added to the daily routines of reservists' lives. While "stress exposure training offers trainees a realistic preview of stress on the battlefield as well as strategies for minimizing the consequences [...] and maintaining performance" (Herz & Wolf, 2010, p. 11). "In [another] study, rats subjected to continual stress became stuck in habitual and ineffective patterns, making it difficult for them to get their basic needs met; once the stressors [...] were removed, the rats were able to regain sufficient concentration and clarity to function (Dias-Ferreira et al., 2009)" (Kottler & Chen, 2011, p. 31).

Monthly training in the NOSC should not be comparable to the training at the RTC or the Academy, nor should it replace the training necessary after re-activation and before deployment. Instead, the monthly training should be designed to maintain military-life culture, as well as the essential operational activities carried out by troops on active duty who have the same military occupational specialties (MOSs)[14] or rates.

The drill climate in the NOSC should focus more on administrative activities than on the actual practice of war tactics, unless that is encompassed in the particular job of a specific reservist. If necessary, such stratagems should be integrated into the activities they conduct during the two weeks of Annual Training (AT)[15]. In a sense, the drills at the NOSC should resemble the coaching or training in the civilian world; although, such training should always be within the outlines of the laws and regulations within the Uniform Code of Military Justice (UCMJ)[16] (Byrne, 1981).

Statement of Problem

In general, when talking about personal tensions with respect to employment, one is referring directly to stress in the workplace, either at a military or civilian installation. Citing the World Health Organization (WHO)[17]: "Work-related stress is the response people may have when presented with work demands and pressures that are not matched to their knowledge and abilities" (WHO, n.d.) and thus challenge their ability to cope.

Numerous studies have shown that these job burdens are by far the greatest source of stress among adults in the United States. According to the American Institute of Stress[18], statistically, this has increased progressively over the first decades of the twenty-first century. Reports about stress in the workplace in the United States reflect not only decreases in the attainment of performance objectives, but a reduction in health status, which is manifested primarily in depressions[19] among those who work under high levels of stress like military personel and police officers within Public Offices in the United States.

In the words of Nicholas Henry (2013) in his textbook *Public Administration and Public Affairs,* the "public authorities function in an astonishingly unconstrained environment. They often have vague geographic boundaries, and may lack a specific constituency" (p. 382). Furthermore, he stated that "to "accomplish" their convoluted and ill-defined mission, public administrators must confront many more "conflicting environmental demands" and "external stakeholders" than [...] managers" (Henry, 2013, p. 93). Ideas that only lead to the function of Supervision, and even more when he concluded as lesson learned that public administrators should "give all employees the opportunity to grow and develop" (p. 93). In a way, this is one of the ideas of high support in supervision that it will be visited later on this essay. Besides, Shulman (2010) already stated that "supervisors usually raise [management] issues when explaining why they cannot be available to their workers as much as they would like" (Shulman, 2010, p. 39), a situation that only create job stress in the workplace.

This work-related stress is cited in a large number of complaints in medical centers and hospitals, including public, private and VA hospitals. There are several conditions associated with these high levels of anxiety, for example: increased blood pressure; depression and other psychosomatic disorders[20], such as asthma; eczema; back pain; migraine; insomnia, and stomach ulcers. In addition, to cope with stress, people develop addictions such as alcoholism, smoking, and drug abuse, among others.

Further, there are other implications besides those relating to health, such as reduced performance, which translates into lower revenues in the private sector or oversights that affect national security among military counterparts. There also is the fact that anxiety and work pressures are having effects on the health of more employees at lower positions in the hierarchy. This evidence alone should prompt organizations to review their supervisory and administrative policies and practices to determine how stress is affecting their employees.

Although different organizations have attempted to compile a list of both the most demanding and the least stressful occupations, these classifications need to be analyzed from the personal perspective of the workers. There could be divergent outcomes defined by situations and people's perceptions of how well they perform a work-related task [highlighting stressful conditions]. For example, working under some pressure can enhance the effectiveness of some, while, at the same time, such pressure can lead to the collapse of another's career. These personal differences must be part of the equation when choosing among different supervisory styles in the workplace. A savvy supervisor must recognize that it is both, the task and the individual adjustment to the work environment that may truly impact the ambiance[21] or climate of the workplace.

In large cities like New York and Los Angeles, the correlation between work stress and heart attacks has already been established. Jurisprudence[22] now includes, for example, regulations when a police officer suffers a coronary[23] failure, either inside or outside the workplace. The statutory law assumes that this is closely related to intrinsic elements of the individual's occupation. Thus, the law has established compensation for heart attacks that occurs when police officers are fishing, on vacation or playing basketball with their neighborhood friends, and "even if the attack occurred at home. Leigh and Miller (1998b)" (Leigh, 2000, p. 210).

Purpose of Study

In light of all the previous considerations of the effects of stress on individuals' operational capabilities, one must consider the vital role played by the military reserve in the country's national security, as well as the ambiance or climate in the workplace, because it can have a direct influence on the health of employees, both civilian and military. This study was designed to determine how these factors interact when reservists are exposed to stress exerted not only by the inherent conditions of the workplace or the work itself, but by management or supervisory styles as well.

Accordingly, this research focused primarily on identifying whether or not there are sources of stress in reservists' training sites. This was delimited specifically to reservists serving in Central (Syracuse) and Western (Buffalo and Rochester) New York state. The research was confined to an analysis of the previous fiscal year, from October 2013 to September 2014. It considered further whether there was any relationship between different supervisory styles and workplace stress. The goal was not simply to identify the problem *per se*[24], but to determine how supervisory styles could affect the climate in the reservists' workplace.

Significance of Study

The wars the United States has fought in the past two decades have yielded a large number of sailors who are afflicted by physical and emotional trauma related to the in-theater missions in which they were involved. Many young sailors have learned how to bear the burden of their trauma, and have decided to continue serving in the ranks of the U.S. Military Reserve. Notwithstanding, stresses in the workplace or the reserve centers are another factor that has affected and challenged their mental health.

Recent testimonies from numerous neurologists and trauma surgeons involved in the medical care of the wave of soldiers returning from the wars in Iraq and Afghanistan have offered a new perspective on this topic. In recent years, researchers have ranked military occupations as "one of the most stressful occupations in human practice" (Mannitz, 2012, p. 271).

According to the varied studies conducted after the Iraq/Afghanistan wars, the stress suffered by soldiers derives not only from their bellicose[25] missions or the physical rigors and dangers of being in those wars. It derived equally from the long absences from their families and the "struggle to remake their 'normal' lives after serving in the war. The transition from military service back to civilian life is not easy, and many Iraq and Afghanistan war veterans have struggle[d] with the physical and emotional scars of war" (Uradnik, Johnson, & Hower, 2011, p. 398).

Furthermore, for those serving in the reserve, there is a constant and disruptive transitional stress that results from reservists and their families knowing that they can be activated at any time. Their civilian employers understand similarly that their businesses could be affected in the event of such mobilizations. These uncertainties in both aspects of the lives of reservists do not leave much room to breathe, and thus they live under the constant pressures imposed by their commanders and civilian employers, or by their perceptions of such pressures.

The civil-military hybrid[26] life of a reservist has not received enough attention until recently, when researchers have begun to understand, in a more detailed way, their specific problems. To fill part of this gap, this study represents a significant endeavor to understand the unique interrelationship between directive styles and the stress endured by U.S. reservists drilling in the NOSCs.

Moreover, this study could be beneficial to other scholars interested in learning about the different ways in which stress interacts with the effectiveness of the supervisory styles used to train military personnel. By understanding the needs of the soldiers and the benefits of a quality climate for drilling activities, this project could in addition provide relevant references to the general audience interested in this topic.

Chapter II: Review of Related Literature

Opening Comments

There is so much written about stress that the researcher has carefully dissected the references used in his study. He decided to opt for studies that have focused in the subjects in their social dimension, and specifically inside organizations. He decided so, because the life of the reservist in the military is like a revolving door, where one day opens to their civilian occupations, and the next day opens to their military duties. In other words, no stopping the cyclical course of their life contrasts.

Paradoxically (given the large number of published papers and studies about stress), it is important to emphasize that the writer could not find another similar study. None was comparable to how supervisory styles impact stress on military personnel in the United States Naval Reserve. That is why the researcher turned to studies about issues in the lives of armed forces personnel instead. Likewise, to studies on how leadership styles affect the lives of the militaries, to correlate those findings to the supervisory approach in the NOSCs of the US Navy Reserve.

In a way, the management and leadership concepts relate to supervision and even when they have much in common; they have some important differences. In general, a high-ranking officer, as well as a corporative manager; they both can establish leadership in many ways without being supervisors. Nevertheless, adroit supervisors have excellent leadership dexterity. In like manner, high-level executives or officers often have great leadership skills and those qualities of effective supervisors.

Now, when it comes to stablish the interaction between the military and public administration, this writer referred to Chris L. Jefferies, PhD. former Major at the U.S. Force Academy: "the armed services are public agencies as well as departments of the Executive Branch of national government and thus fall within the milieu of public administration" (1977, p. 322). On his essay, *Public Administration and the Military*, Jefferies cited the political-sociologist scientist Samuel Huntington, who addresses the possibility of the phenomenon by pointing out that:

> Political involvement of military leadership takes two forms: (1) espousing and recommending policies derived from non-military sources, unrelated or contrary to the professional military viewpoint, in which case they assume a substantive political role; and (2) playing an active part in the public defense or merchandising of policies before Congress and the public. In these political roles, military officers have […] explained the Administration's decision on forces levels and budgets [subtracting form other public offices like Education and Social Services]. (Jefferies, 1977, p. 330).

Considering all these factors previously presented, the studies annotated by the writer in this literary review included some medical and biological studies related to stress. He also incorporated treatises[27] examining military interaction with public administration, as well as, the sociological problems of military personnel. For example, there are studies reflecting upon when militaries are transferring from active duty to civilian life, or to a kind of moonlight[28] military life. He also added studies on supervision as well as leadership's styles, and their relation to operational performances. It is important to mention that some of the studies were included due to its historical reference milestone, and others, to trace the evolution in the different approaches to the study of stress.

Review and Critique of Literature

As mentioned before, several pieces have been written to understand stress and specifically this in the workplace; including those about civilians and militaries. These publications started mainly in the early eighties when the Organizational Culture flourished and boomed. As Ravasi and Schultz (2006) defined it, this was the set of shared mental assumptions that guide interpretations and actions in organizations, as they must be implemented by defining appropriate behavior for various situations (Ravasi & Schultz, 2006).

In any case, the apprehension of stress causes and effects is still a very subjective phenomenon due to the uniqueness of each human being. One can argue that stress varies depending upon specific circumstances or unique conflictive conditions in a particular lifestyle, personal predispositions or just the social status[29] of the subjects.

Scholars worldwide have evolved, adapted and developed fresh, renewed and fascinating or just mesmeric[30] ways to quantify stress. For example, the famous neuroendocrinologist Robert Sapolsky has studied the animals' chemical reactions to stress in the natural environment of baboons[31] in Kenya, Africa (Sapolsky, 2002, p. 312). More specifically, he has conducted an innovative biochemical analysis of the cortisol[32] levels between the alpha[33] males and females and their subordinates to determine their stress levels according to their hierarchical social positions.

Sir Michael G. Marmot, professor of Epidemiology and Public Health at the University College of London, conducted ground-breaking research for the Whitehall[34] studies of British Civil Servants[35] published in 2006. This is the United Kingdom's oldest governmental organization from which Americans copied most of its organizational structures for their Civil Services agencies. These studies "aimed to determine the relationship between social status and health" (Reid, 2009, p. 166).

These studies by Sapolsky and Marmot are a great help in analyzing the conditions of civilians or those in the military. Like the social workers at Whitehall in London, the hierarchical position within the military equally and directly influences the staff's health conditions. Clearly, those in the higher ranks are in advantageous positions, giving that they have more control over their tasks, and so they experience less stress than those in lower ranks. In contrast, those in the lowest ranks have less control over their jobs and much more supervision, which tends to increase their stress levels.

Other scholars have argued that the presences or perception of stress in the armed forces workplace could be, among other causes, the response to factors like the established institutional policies and practices or just the military culture (Karney & Crown, 2007, p. 170). Additionally, stress could be affected by the way operational tasks are perceived or unofficially implemented, giving that no matter the organization, one can always find "unwritten rules" of operations.

According to Guy P. Fehr; there are unwritten rules in every workplace. You won't find them in policy or procedure manuals or job descriptions, yet they directly impact the success and effectiveness of every manager or supervisor. These unwritten rules exist in every company or organization; as the informal ways things are done [or not], and the most important, things to watch for or be aware of in a particular organization. They are not spelled out officially; so, "unless you are fortunate enough to have, or have had a savvy mentor, the unwritten rules are usually learned the hard way, after they have been broken or ignored" (Fehr, 2010, p. xi).

It is also obvious that other external conditions are especially influential for reservists' stress. Factors such as unemployment and changes in the political and government arenas, or relate to who control the number of their hard billets[36] (the regular remunerative military positions). Those have been recognized and isolated by this researcher in order to focus this study more on the context of the workplace.

Medical/Biological Definitions of Stress

William R. Lovallo, in his book, *Stress and Health: Biological and Psychological Interactions,* provides a clear image of stress from the interactive genetics and behavioral points of view, which are perspectives that apply to civilians or military subjects. In his book, he does a splendid job of filling the gap in the literature about how stress and health are related in a scientific way. He elaborates on an introductory compendium that integrates what is known in physiology about stress and then combines it with the human biological process. This approach was widely used by the biologist Sapolsky in his studies of stress in primates in 2002.

The material in the second edition of his book is useful for a better understanding of the mechanisms of "how our mind and psychosocial factors affect the states of health and diseases when confronted with external stimulus" (Lovallo, 2005, p. 282). Lovallo opened up the dialogue with the definition of "stress as a bodily or mental tension resulting from factors that tend to alter an existent equilibrium (Merriam-Webster's Collegiate Dictionary, 1993)" (Lovallo, 2005, p. 29). On one hand, he explains how the central nervous system controls stress by hormone secretions. On the other hand, he covers a topic about the genes[37] and explains how they shape the stress responses. These reactions create the vulnerabilities responsible for snapping the normal steadiness of human beings.

Lovallo noted that the definition of stress has two elements. First, there is tension, presumably caused by some force pulling on the nervous system. Second, this tension is a threat to the normal equilibrium of the system. These two elements tell us that the stress is an active process that involves personal genetics and reacts via external factors or actions outside the internal human system and threatens its equilibrium. It is assumed that the tension may cause harm unless some process of compensation reduces the disequilibrium to a baseline level or until the cause is removed. For example, the commands from a supervisor or the settings in the workplace are good examples of external factors that could cause stress and upset the natural equanimity[38]. Along these lines, the researcher asked the reservists directly about the clarity of their supervisor's communications and if the operational structure was equally explained in detail.

Stress and Operational Performances

Thomas W. Britt and Carl A. Castro are other important authors who have greatly contributed to learning how stress relates and interacts with the operations or performances of military personnel. In four volumes, these authors tell their narratives about the lives and sacrifices of military personnel. They start with their performances before getting into the causes and effects of operational stress. They explain how the U.S. armed forces are confronted with combat missions resulting from the nation's global commitments. According to them, men and women in the military are faced with challenges that threaten their lives or those of others on a daily basis on the battlefield. Per contra[39], once they are back at home, less visible threats affect their mental health, man or woman, whether they are in the active or reserve components of the armed forces.

In volume two, they highlight the factors that help the members of the armed forces to develop a state of greater strength than ordinary citizens. They explain how, "traditionally, military training has focused on skills development" (Driskell et al., Volume I; Keinan & Friedland, 1996), beginning with a knowledge component that is provided during lectures and briefings (Thompson & Pasto, 2003). Demonstrations and drills emphasize technical proficiency, discipline, strength, [and] endurance" (Britt, Adler, & Castro, 2006, p. 56).

In their four volumes, they describe the programs and practices used to alleviate the psychological burdens of military personnel and their families and children. In volume two, they focus on the psychological factors facing military service men and women in times of war and peace, as well as the operational stress on these soldiers' lives. Despite their extraordinary efforts to explain this operational stress, the authors do not analyze the relationship between stress and supervisory styles confronted by the reservists at their training centers.

Johnson and Doyle added that it is obvious, even when away from home, that the soldiers have to raise their children, sometimes as single parents. Sadly, the children often get caught in the middle of this dilemma and have to learn what it feels like to be in a military family, and they have to make sense of the separation of their parents when their parents are on active military missions or in training (Johnson & Doyle, 2010, p. 253). With these considerations, the authors based their studies on reflections from psychologists, psychiatrists, counselors, and coaches to try to explain what happens inside the mind of the military personnel when confronted with bigger challenges than those that appear in the news headlines.

Stress in a Social Dimension

With support from *Discover* magazine[40] (Garfield, 1981), in 2002 Sapolsky went on a tour of seven cities to attract readers' attention to the most interesting parts of the animal world in Africa and to promote ecology globally. Scientists at the University of North Carolina, the University of London, Rockefeller University, and the University of California at San Francisco joined in this effort. They all have their points of view about how stress is figuratively "killing" people, thus giving new relevance to the study of stress and the need to understand the major role it is playing on directly affecting our lives in an increasingly more complex society.

In Marmot (2004) publication, *The Status Syndrome*, he corroborated Sapolsky's findings and demonstrated that the same conditions in primates' societies apply to organizations of public administration. More, he demonstrated how one's social standing directly affects health and life expectancy (M. G. Marmot, 2004, p. 184). He argued that just like the hierarchical levels in primates' social orders, a person's socio-economic position is an important factor influencing health conditions.

Later on his book, *Why Care?:how status affects our health and longevity*, Marmot (2006) touched on the fundamental factors to consider in any investigation that aims to determine how hierarchal positions affect animals' and humans' performance. This is, without a doubt, the best starting point to understand how stress intertwines with the different positions within the hierarchical scheme of any organization (M. Marmot, 2006).

Another condition in the social dimension that can affect stress is the sense of emptiness and hopelessness among those who do not seem to find their personal place in society. On this account, Prociuk, Breen, and Lussier (1976) came out with a study that examined the relationship between hopelessness[41], defined as a system of negative expectancies about the future, and two theoretically relevant constructs: internal-external locus of control[42], and depression. They supported the predictions that hopelessness would be positively related to an external locus of control and to depression (Prociuk, Breen, & Lussier, 1976).

As Philip Zimbardo (1985) addressed it, when one is dealing with challenges and feels that the control is out of one's hands, this is an external locus issue. According to him, "'A locus of control orientation is a belief about whether the outcomes of our actions are contingent on what we do (internal control orientation) or on events outside our personal control (external control orientation) " (Zimbardo, 1985, p. 275). This total lack of control over the future is one of the main reasons for those hopelessness feelings, which can trigger intense stress, as well as, depression. These inferring factors of stress were considered in this study and addressed in the Item #38, Q.30.

Stress in the Workplace

In 2004, Marmot published, *The Status Syndrome*. In this book, he presented mixed research with only a few graphs related to statistical content. To his credit, he provides an overview of the current understanding of how our health depends on the society around us. He also mentioned the sense of autonomy and control one has over one's life. Based on his research, Marmot made policy recommendations to the World Health Council[43] (Foege, 2005), among others. His work is, therefore, very revealing material about how employees should review their stance towards the way their jobs are manipulating their health.

Following the works of Sapolsky and Marmot, National Geographic[44] produced a documentary about stress in 2008. This video examines how positions in the workplace and society are affecting our lives. This documentary presents a parallel between the humans' positions in the social hierarchy of the Homo-sapiens[45] compared to the animal kingdom. After all, humans are still within the animals' kingdom, and some are "apparently" more irrationals than others. Anyhow, this documentary is a must for anyone who intends to study how hierarchy affects animals and humans (National_Geography, 2008).

Supervisory vs. Leadership Styles

When scrutinizing the history of administration, one realize that the supervisor position was created in the factories during the Industrial Revolution[46]. In those days, supervisors were assigned to control the production of the workers during their long working hours. Later, this role and the term were adopted by service providers and even military institutions. Supervisors, in a much-synthesized way, are the link between high management and those in the base positions doing the *labour* or productive physical activities of the organization.

While supervisors have the primary task to control, they need to know how to guide and provide support and solidarity to their subordinates or subalterns[47]. This viewpoint of this small task is similar to what is expected from good leadership. This particular function is considered as the set of managerial skills that an individual has to have to influence a particular person or groups, causing them to work with enthusiasm in achieving specific goals and objectives. This is the essential difference between these two tasks or functions.

In 2002, Bekkers and Homburg published a paper in which both authors analyzed these sometimes contradictory roles of administrative supervisors, demanding and inspiring, and the implications for their functional or informational relationships. In addition, they touched on the consequences associated to practices with each one of the different roles that a supervisor assumes (Bekkers, 2002). None of these particular functions was related to military operations, yet they still provided a clear idea about the behavior of those carrying out these functions. After all, the reservists are between the two worlds of civilians and the military.

In 2010, Professor Lawrence Shulman published a book from his studies in 1981 and 1991 about supervision in the social services in the United States in which he talked about the stress inflicted by bad supervisory practices like not being available to their workers for consultations or teaching roles (Shulman, 2010, pp. 39-40). He devoted much of his time to the study of how supervision affects the lives of workers in public services. He presented a variety of real-life cases to illustrate theoretically how the practice itself is orienting the scientific work in social services. In the book, he provided many of the tools he has used in his research, and these were of great value, given their proven practicality. In this paper, this researcher used, with the consented permission of the author (Figure #2), parts of some of the questions he used during his studies, which he published later in his textbook, *Interactional Supervision* (Shulman, 2010).

Dealing specifically with the tasks of overseeing and directing others, there is a dissertation that deserves special attention. In 2005, Terry Gatfield from the Griffith University in Australia, in his "Investigation into Ph.D. Supervisory Management Styles" proposed four main approaches based on a model using "support and structure." For this purpose, he used the horizontal axis to represent the "structure" and the vertical axis to represent "support" as presented in the Chart #1 (Gatfield, 2005, p. 319). Based on this model, the writer of this paper used these same parameters to measure the different supervisory styles in the Naval Operational Support Centers (NOSCs; Chart #1).

Chart #1: Adapted from Gatfield, T. (2005) Supervisory Management Styles.

High Support	Pastoral Style	Contractual Style
	-Low structure and high support	-High structure and high support
	-[Reservist] has personal low management skill but	-[Reservist] highly motivated and able to take

	takes advantage of all the support facilities that are on offer -Supervisor provides considerable personal care and support but not necessarily in a task-driven, directive capacity	direction and to act on own initiative -Supervisor able to administer direction and exercises good management skills and interpersonal relationships
Low Support	Laissez-faire Style	Directorial Style
	-Low structure low support -[Reservist] has limited levels of motivation and management skills -Supervisor in non-directive and not committed to high levels of personal interaction -Supervisor may appear uncaring and uninvolved	-High structure and low support -[Reservist] highly motivated and sees the necessity to take advantage of engaging in high structural activities such as setting objectives, completing and submitting work on time on own initiative without taking advantage of institutional support -Supervisor has a close and regular interactive relationship with the candidate, but avoids non-task issues
	Low Structure	High Structure

Stress impact of Supervisory Styles

Based on Gatfield approach, Eley and Murray came out with a new perspective when talking about "Supervising effectively." They established that "there is debate about what constitutes 'effective' supervision;" yet, they emphasized the following five basic points:

• "An effective supervisor can change his or her practice over time, as [progresses develops]" unlike in the military, since any change involves a slow process full of discussions and multiple approvals.

• "Supervision may be different for each [person] and [each] may have different expectations." In the military services in the United States, every soldier is treated basically the same. The reason is to avoid any perception of favoritism, which may affect the overall morale of the service members and officers.

• "Defining supervision may involve explaining what the supervisor will - and will not – do." This is only partially true, since there are situations in combat that can only be considered from their particular circumstances.

• "Taking account of individual differences may involve adjusting the style of supervision." This could apply to freedom of action that can be given for the execution of a particular task. Besides, all members working on similar tasks cannot expect more than the same treatment.

• "Providing structure and prompting […] to plan are critical tasks for supervisors," which is an impossible consideration in the military, since the plans are given from the highest spheres. Certainly, the freedom to maneuver is limited since it is associated with the resources allocated to each particular task. (Eley & Murray, 2009, p. 54)

In 2005, Delini M. Fernando and Diana Hulse-Killacky published a paper on "The Relationship of Supervisory Styles to Satisfaction with Supervision and the Perceived Self-Efficacy of Master's-Level Counseling Students" (Fernando & Hulse-Killacky, 2005). This work, not related to military activities at all, masterfully focuses on how supervisory styles directly relate to stress. Actually, one of the questions in this research came directly from one of the comments on their paper. They clearly stated: "Previous research (Friedlander & Snyder, 1983) found that supervisees expect supervisors to have an impact on their personal […] developmental needs" (p. 300). This is in a way the query 23 (Table #23) in regard to question #15 of this writer's questionnaire (Appendix E p.2)

Later in 2007, Buelens and Broeck presented a research study that raised questions about the importance of the work-life-balance (W-L-B) in regard to how to improve operational performances[48]. The study also made an interesting point when the authors reflected upon the hierarchies in the public sector, which is the major consideration of Marmot studies about the civil service employees in the United Kingdom (Buelens, 2007). Moreover, some of the questions in this study touched directly on how reservist perceived their particular W-L-B affecting their levels of stress, based on their own perspectives of what should be a good balance.

In 2008, Rogers studied police entities as a component of the social structures of public administration. He recognized that these organizations increasingly recognize the role of leadership. It is therefore important to understand and spend some time in all levels of the government hierarchies, including groups of police officers, who are significantly involved in assisting the public in their communities (Rogers, 2008). The researcher looked into this social assimilation of policing as part of public administration to compare it against the attitudes of other public employees of other government agencies (including the military) to understand better how the government is affecting the civic lives of the reservists. In any case, there are a large number of policemen in the military rows as reservists.

This is a common practice; in America most reservists tend to seek jobs in public offices. In this sense, their dual roles as military and public servants often lead them to take positions of leadership in their civilian occupations that do not reflect their military lives, in which they only follow orders. Unfortunately, this writer could not correlate how these two spheres of life of the reservists intertwine in relation to stress. Still, this is an interesting point for future research.

Afterward, in an essay from 2013, Green and Krasikova explained some destructive practices in supervision. They addressed some ambiguities about the nature of deadly leadership. They made it explicit, to a certain degree, how some characteristics of inadequate leadership are differentiated from other forms of good leading, such as leading by example. Later, they integrated this thinking into a theoretical model in which they explained the manifestations of destructive leadership and its antecedents and consequences (Green & Krasikova, 2013). Based on these models, the writer adopted some of the issues presented by them in their research in a question about how the example of the supervisor influences the motivation of the soldiers.

Finally, thanks to the work of M. Wofford, one can get, to a greater degree, the necessary information to sort the truly touchy way of those whose profiles and patterns are foreign to the general public's way of thinking and being. Hopefully, one can be a more fortunate person as a result of being better equipped to recognize the clashing of profiles versus the truly difficult personalities (Wofford, 2012). In essence, this book is a good source to diagnose people in the workplace and recognize what percentages are avoiding others, or simply, what percentage may be suffering from social anxiety [49]. This work mainly attracted this writer's attention about social-life topics and factors that can affect the stress of reservists in their military and civilian lives. Therefore, it served to eliminate obvious questions about stressful worries, which were mostly about politics and government. It also helped to define those with toxic social personalities that are not so obvious at firsthand.

Summary of Literature Review

The studies about stress presented by medicine doctors and biologists like Michael Marmot and Robert Sapolsky have amply demonstrated the negative aspects of stress in modern social organizations. Sadly, their theories could not be verified by the researcher, given the limited involvement of high-ranking officers in the study. In later conversations with a few of them, some commented that it could not be necessarily the position of the soldiers, rather the management style of the commander. Still, is this not, in essence, what it means to have control? Those on higher position have certainly better control over their actions, as well as greater ability to control the actions of those they supervise, as is the case of the commanders.

Meanwhile, other authors, such as the psychiatrist William Robert Lovallo, have subsequently confirmed how biological and genetic factors influence the way a person is affected by stress. Although he recognized that external factors play an important role in affecting the human's internal mechanism of equanimity, those external factors such as the structure of the organization or the support extended by supervisors were the aspects that the writer evaluated in this study.

In another vein of ideas, the scholar Terry Gatfield, who has studied the critical directing functions, offered the necessary stroke to draw a parallel between supervisory styles and stress. In his studies about coaching and directing Ph.D. students, he proposed four main styles of supervision. These were based on a model that used "support" and "structure," which the researcher utilized to develop the present study on how supervisory styles affect stress in a reserve center in Central New York.

Workplace stress affects the physical and mental health of workers and leads to increasing injuries and illnesses. This work-related stress interferes with the body's cardiac rhythm and mental depression, resulting in increased injury rates, psychosocial problems[50], and physical health problems (including psychosomatic issues with negligible appearances like listening problems or sleeping disorders). Workers with stress disorder-related issues tend to gravitate towards unemployment sooner rather than later, either in the civilian or military spheres. Therefore, it is obvious that there is a need to reduce stressors in the workplace and help employees control the individual and external factors that are directly related to their operational performances.

In the active military arena, there are a fair number of essays on how the different types of leadership influence or impact stress. Equally, many research studies about the issues in the life of active soldiers have been written. Yet, there are few and scattered studies on the training environment of the military reservists. Lamentably, very few studies look at how their double lives as civilians and military personnel intertwine and almost none discuss how the spillover of one sphere over the other relates to the stressful factors in their lives. Evidently, by the number of members in this population, the interested audience is relatively small, and the military culture has not allowed more access to study this small component of the military forces due to issues of confidentiality and the secrecy of military missions by the United States of America around the world.

It is true that the lives of the ready combatants were rather boring in the past. Even so, today they are an essential part of the active military forces of the nation and with a more operative role increasing every day. They have shown to be always ready to engage at any time whenever the country needs their services or duties. These new circumstances are taking them to similar stress levels of those other components that are on continuous active duty. Whereas all these reasons now make the military reservists a more important study subject, it was the purpose of this researcher to open the dialogue about how supervisory styles relate to stress among military reservists in the United States.

Chapter III: Methodology

Design of Study

After compiling the literary review, the researcher decided on the objectives, formulated some hypotheses, and defined the main information needed to test or explain the occurrence of the specified targeted problem. In this sense, the dependent variable of the study was "stress," the empirically observable phenomenon capable or likely to change. This variable was

analyzed as a function of the "supervisory styles," which was the

independent variable.

To correlate these two, or to understand their reciprocal

relation, there were two conceptual ideas or theories that needed to be

proved. These two postulates were the central focus of attention

throughout this study. The first was the null hypothesis, and the second

was the working hypothesis. In addition, another three premises were

considered as alternative causes of stress. These were correlated to

unfair practices of treating others that have been proven to affect the

healthy mental state of a person, like harassment, bullying[51], and

discrimination.

- Null Hypothesis (H_0): There is no significant statistical correlation

  between stress and the supervisory styles in place at the Naval

  Operational Support Centers.

- Working Hypothesis (H_1): There is a significant statistical correlation

  between stress and the supervisory styles in place at the Naval

  Operational Support Centers.

- Alternative Hypothesis one (H_{a1}): There is a significant statistical correlation between stress and the harassment taking place at the Naval Operational Support Centers.

- Alternative Hypothesis two (H_{a2}): There is a significant statistical correlation between stress and the bullying taking place at the Naval Operational Support Centers.

- Alternative Hypothesis three (H_{a3}): There is a significant statistical correlation between stress and the discrimination taking place at the Naval Operational Support Centers.

Within this design, first-hand information was obtained through a questionnaire given to the Ready Reservists drilling at the Naval Operational Support Center in Syracuse in the central region of the State of New York. As for the tabulation of the inputs obtained, this writer decided to use the Online Survey Software & Insight Platform, Qualtrics[52]. By the same token, the secondary sources included data from many censuses of military records and other published research about military affairs. This information provided an opportunity to explore materials from recent and more distant periods of time to gain insights into both for methodological and theoretical purposes.

Regarding the structure of the questionnaire, the 40 different entries on two pages had the first eight questions related to demographics. The following 31 were close-ended questions, with four or five Likert options. The organization of the particular values were ascending for some group or set of questions and deliberately altered to a descending order to stimulate the alertness of the interviewees. Ten questions targeted stress indicators directly, another sixteen the supervisory style, another five specific behavioral unfair treatments to others, and an open-ended question was for comments as the last entry or item in the questionnaire.

One last topic about the design refers to the different stages followed in this research. This project was implemented in five stages. The first was the collection, review, and evaluation of the secondary data, which was covered in the literary review portion of this report. It was also necessary to verify the accuracy of all the information obtained and the credentials of the authors in the references of this study. The second was the development and distribution of the questionnaire to be completed by military reservists and their supervisors drilling at the Naval Operational Support Centers. The third was the invitation to comments in order to gather more qualitative insights into the subject matter. The fourth was the analysis and interpretation of all the data collected. The fifth and final was the comparison of the quantitative

and qualitative data to formulate the conclusions of this research study.

Sample Selection

The sample size was designed to include every military reservist in

the target population. On average, 160 to 180 members were in each NOSC

for an approximate total of 500 subjects. With the approval of the COs in

every NOC, everyone was free to decide whether or not to participate in the

study by signing a consent form. The only particular exclusion criterion was

a sailor's openly and expressed unwillingness to take part in the study. No

vulnerable subjects, such as pregnant women or minors, were included in the

sample.

The participants' ages ranged from 18 to 60 years. There were no

special reasons for determining this age range, which are the allowed ages of

sailors in the U.S. Navy Reserve. The general age requirement for the Navy

Reserve is that a person must be at least 18 and could have 20 years of total

service by the age of 60. In like manner, since this institution does not

discriminate on sex, the subjects were both, male and female. There were no

special considerations to any possible variations in the perception of a subject's gender, as now new laws allow the unrestricted participation of homosexuals in the military.

With respect to the number of cases or the sample size, the researcher tried to include the total number of reservists drilling at the targeted centers. He tried to have them all participate because including all service members and supervisors only raised the total size of the population to approximately 500. This was the number of sailors at that time in the three different NOSCs in Buffalo and Rochester in Western New York, and Syracuse in Central New York. Evidently, this number of cases did not demand too many resources; all that was needed was the reproduction of 500 copies of the questionnaire on both sides and its transportation and collection from the respective reserve centers.

An important factor that this writer never considered was the enormous challenge represented by the willingness of the participants and the authorities to engage and allow the study. These two factors were responsible for reducing the final size of the population to approximately 110 participants in only the NOSC Syracuse in Central New York. This reduced number of reservists was due to mainly two inherent factors at this center. First, one of the largest units that were drilling there, the Seabees[53] got decommissioned. Second, the center was going through renovations to the main building, and all their activities and staffs were reduced to operating in 5 trailers of different sizes, which included sanitary facilities.

Now, focusing on the issue of how to avoid inaccuracies resulting from the sample size, the researcher based the study on the margin of error formula from The Research Advisors or Fowler's (2009) suggested tables (Appendix F).

$$SS = X2 * N * P * (1\text{-}P) / (ME2 * (N\text{-}1) + (X2 * P * (1\text{-}P))). \; X2 =$$

Chi-square

Confidence level at 1 degree of freedom; N = Population Size; P = Population Proportion at .50; ME = Margin of Error (expressed as a proportion).

In this sense, considering the total population of 110 at the NOSC Syracuse during the study, the sample size should have consisted of 86 reservists. Because there were 12 service members on special assignments, a few others absent, and around 25 to 30 in the spotlight or going through different stations to prove their availability and readiness for mobilization, the actual number of reservists available to participate in the research was reduced to 70 sailors. Under these restrictive conditions, the sample size needed was met with 59 participants based on the following considerations: a confidence level[54] of 95%, and a confidence interval[55] of five points.

Data Collection Method

This research study involved the collection of information from primary and secondary sources. It utilized a mixed-methods approach for compiling objective and subjective data. Since in a qualitative study to process the statistical information about the behavior within an organization becomes very strenuous, this research profited from the efficacy of the quantitative approach through the use of a questionnaire. While benefiting from the in-depth insights of secondary information and an open-ended question for comments among the queries, the results were linked at the end with the efficiency of the quantitative analysis.

The questionnaire was pilot-tested for reliability in one of the units drilling at NOSC Syracuse in New York. The researcher verified that each question answered to one of the variables established and that all the objectives were covered by the questions asked. The result of the pilot-test showed consistency with the study objectives and a clear interpretation of the formulation of the queries and the set of Likert selected. Thus, the instruments proved to be easy to follow and reliable (Appendix E: p.1 & p.2).

Likewise, according to protocols and before distributing the survey, the researcher asked the reservists to express voluntarily their desire to participate in the study by signing an Informed Consent Form (Appendix D). This form was previously approved by the Institutional review Board[56] [IRB] at SUNY Buffalo State, in consonance with the Site Agreements (Appendix A, B, and C) that the NOSCs signed to allow the collection of information through this questionnaire.

For qualitative data, the researcher included an open-ended question in the questionnaire. Further, he welcomed and stimulated discussions and comments from all the participants. As a result of these conversations, two comments were received by email. In addition, a variety of documents such as books, essays, reports and statistical analysis in magazines, and other school publications, as well as the Internet, were analyzed. All these were relevant documents related to stress, supervisory styles, and the military life of reservists.

Data Analysis

After the collection of the questionnaires, the data gathered for the study were computer-processed for its statistical analysis using the Qualtrics

Online Survey Software. The descriptive statistics employed were means,
variances, and standard deviations. The statistical test employed to
demonstrate the independence between variables was a chi-square.

From the report's section obtained through the Qualtric's statistics
software, the researcher compiled the following data analysis.

Demographics (Tables 1-8):

(1) Age: The significant average age of the participant sailors ranges
from 26 to 35; this average represents 51% of the sample population. There
were 16% below 26 years, and 33% above 35 years of age.

(2) Sex: Males represent 80% of population and females the other
20%, which mean 1 of every 5 sailors were women.

(3) Ethnicity: 89% of sailors were White and 11% of other
ethnicities; including Latinos, African descendants, Native Americans, and
Asian-Pacific.

(4) Time in service: From 0-5 was 23.64% of the population, 6-10 was 31%, 11-15 was 23.64%, and 16 to 20+ was 22%. The most significant group of time-in-service was the one between 6-10 years in service.

(5) Pay grade – Enlisted: The group of E-4 was 17%, E-5 35%, and E-6 was 29%, under E-4 nearly 10% and over E-6 closely to 10%. The most important group was the one of E-5 with 35% of the population.

(6) Pay grade – Officers: Out of all the sailors in this population, only 4 officers participated, and all of them have a different pay grade ranging from O-1 to O-4.

(7) Time in grade: Between 0-4 years was 64%, 5-8 was 25%, and over 8 years was 11%.

It seems like there have been a lot of new recruits coming into the NOSC in the past 4 years. 2 out of 3 sailors have joined the U.S. Navy Reserve within the last 4 years for this sample of the population in NOSC Syracuse.

(8) Education: 61% of the participants in this research have less than a bachelor's degree. 39% have at least a bachelor's degree.

Stress Indicators (Tables 9-10, 15-16, 22, 31-33, 37-38):

(9-Q1) Mood swing (after leaving the workplace): About 28% did not experience a mood swing last year. In contracts, 21% or nearly 2 out of every 9 sailors have experienced a mood swing every drill-day, all year around. The remaining 51% have experienced it from 1 to 5 times during the past year. It is important to mention that one sailor commented there was a positive mood swing change for him.

(10-Q2) Stress: 81% or about 4 out of every 5 have reported feeling stress in his or her standard drill-day last year. 67% of participants felt stressed from one to four times in a typical drill day. Only 7% of the sample population has felt stressed regularly, every drill day all year around. It is a small percentage, 1 out of every 14; even so, very intense pressure (See Chart #2).

Chart #2:

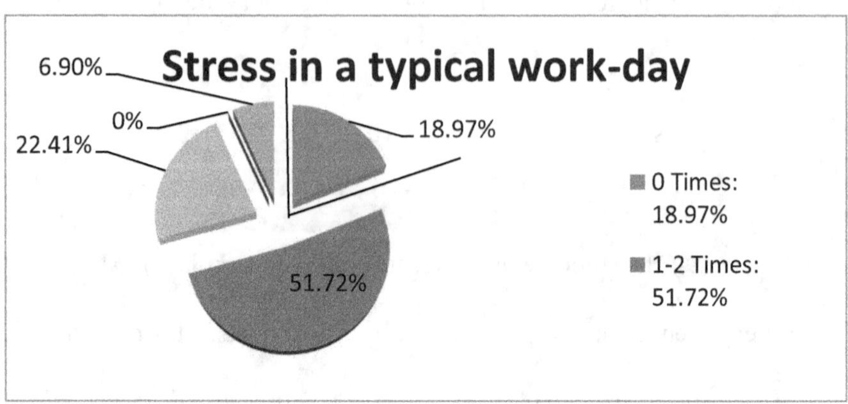

(15-Q7) Autonomy: 93% of participants were moderately satisfied to very-satisfy regarding the autonomy to complete their work

(16-Q8) Reporting: 72% are moderately satisfied to very satisfy with individuals reporting to them.

(22-Q14) Defensive towards the supervisor: 84% from strongly to very strongly disagreed.

(31-Q23) Stress reducing quality: 64% vs. 36%, 2 out of 3 disagree to strongly disagree. So, they do their best no matter the stress.

(32-Q24) Alcohol: 84% disagree to strongly disagree; almost 6 out of 7 do not need alcohol to cup with stress.

(33-Q25) Sleep problems: 77% Disagree to strongly-disagree (no major sleep problems).

(37-Q29) Anger: 86% Disagree to strongly-disagree (no major anger problems).

(38-Q30) No other place to fit-in outside military life: 89% disagree to strongly disagree (they feel good outside military life), and 11% are feeling some difficulties fitting outside their service life.

(39-Q31) Meaningfulness (importance of work): 78% agree to strongly agree (they find meaning in what they are doing, and that motivate them to work).

Specific indicators (harassment, bullying, discrimination, communication and motivation from supervisor – Tables 12-14, 35, 39):

(12-Q4) Harassment: 78% have not felt harassed by their supervisor at all during the past year. 16% have found been harassed 1 or 2 times in a regular drill-day. 5% (3 sailors) have felt harassed from 3 to 5 times in a typical drill-day. Only 1 sailor manifested has felt harassed every drill weekend during the past year. On this regard, just 2 female's members have said felt harassed out of this population sample (ranging from 1 to 4 times). In the same token, merely one male sailor has considered harassed. However, he has felt harassed every drill day or all year around.

(13-Q5) Bullying: 83% reported not felt bullied at all. Nearly 9% reported one incident of bullying in a typical workday; and 5% from 3 to 5 incidents in a standard drill weekend. 3% or 2 sailors have reported felt bullied every drill day during last year.

(14-Q6) Discrimination: 90% have not felt discriminated. Still, 10% have felt some form of discrimination, including one participant that felt discriminated every drill weekend during the past year. This percentage is extremely low, but it is a significant issue given the zero tolerances policy in the U.S. Navy Reserve.

(21-Q13) Communication with the supervisor: 86% communicate from moderately well to very well.

(35-Q27) Supervisor example: 70% agree to strongly agree that his or her supervisor is very inspiring. 30% or 3 out 10 disagree to strongly disagree (supervisor is not very inspiring)

Supervisory Styles (Support vs. Structure – Tables 11, 17-21, 23-30, 34, 36):

(11-Q3) Feedback: 35% of the participants reported no feedback at all from their supervisors in a typical work-day. 45% of the participants reported one or two feedbacks in a regular work-day. 13% or 1 out of 5 members said to receive feedback from 3 to 5 times in a typical work-day. Here are evidences of low support reported by 80% of the sample population due to limited or no feedback from supervision (See Chart #3).

Chart #3:

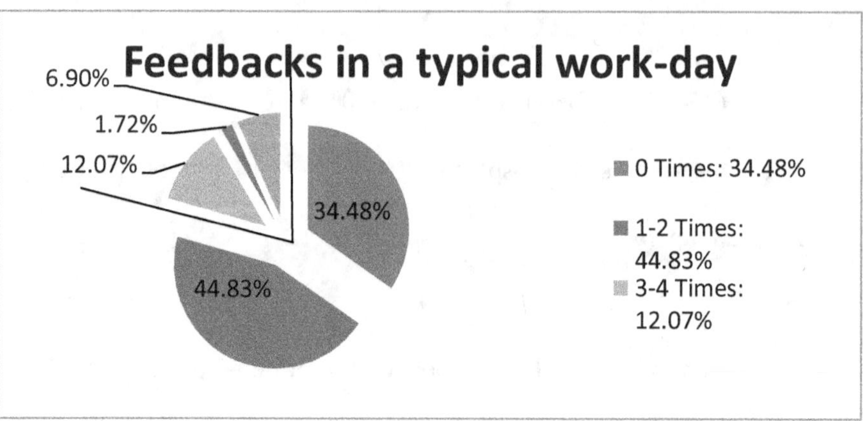

(17-Q9) Sharing responsibility: 83% felt that the responsibilities were equally distributed.

18-10 Mission knowledge: 90% understand the command mission from moderately well to very well.

(19-Q11) Structure: 93% knew their command structure from moderately well to very well.

(20-Q12) Operations: 86% knew it from moderately well to very well.

(23-Q15) Career development: 66% agree to strongly agree that their supervisor has been involved in their individual career development planning.

(24-Q16) Mission explained: 66% stated that their supervisor explained their command mission or 2 out of 3 service members.

(25-Q17) Structure explained: 64% agree to strongly agree vs. 36% that the supervisor clearly described the command's structure at their arrival.

(26-Q18) Operations explained: 62% agree to strongly–agree vs. 38% that the supervisor patently described the command's operations at their arrival.

(27-Q19) What is expected from me: 75% or 3 out of 4 service members knew exactly what was expected from he or she at all times.

(28-Q20) Resources: 64% agree to strongly agree or 2 out of every 3 reservists stated that they had access to the necessary resources to carry out their work.

(29-Q21) Good working relations: 80% (4 out of 5) agree to strongly agree in having good working relations with their supervisors.

(30-Q22) Professional development: 64% agree to strongly agree that their command was contributing on their career development.

(34-Q26) Opportunities: 62% (nearly 3 out of 5) vs. 38% reported from moderately easy to extremely easy that they can find an opportunity to advance their military careers.

(36-Q28) Work pace: 75% or 3 out of 4 agree to strongly agree they stated that the work pace was always reasonable in the workplace.

(40) Comments (Table 40):

-I have experienced positive mood changes.

-I felt stressed due to the lack of hands-on training, not related to supervision.

-I find my command has enabled my success so far and loves the Navy.

Comments from e-mails sent directly to the researcher:

-Being in trailers is not helping with the communications. I think Navy Reservists need a lot more mentoring, and every sailor should have an E-5 or E-6 as a mentor.

- There is an ongoing problem of lack of communication.

- People are finding it hard to advance, and the burden comes from not having particular unit's duties, which leads to poor evaluations, which leads to decreased chance to advance.

- The lack of shared responsibilities is a critical issue because people do not feel their supervisors care when they are not given any responsibilities to them. Despite this, there are only so many unit specific tasks that can be dealt out. I do believe this is a great source of frustration.

Chapter IV: Results, Conclusions, Summary
Results

Based on the descriptive analysis in this study, the most relevant and evident finding was that the reservists in the NOSC Syracuse in Central New York were a very cohesive group. This characteristic refers to their ethnicity, ages, and educational backgrounds. This group has very little diversity in their ranks. In approximate numbers, 75% were between 21 to 40 years of age; 80% were male; 89% were Caucasian; 81% were between the pay grades[57] of E-4 to E-6; 50% had from 1 to 10 years of service; and 56% had either an Associate AA/AS or a Bachelor's degree.

As for their answers to item #10, Q.02, 81% stated having experienced stress during the past fiscal year (October 2013 to September 2014). Even at the stated low levels of one to three times during a typical workday, there was still stress in the workplace. Curiously, from the answers of the interviewees who felt stressed, none corresponded to the officers who participated in the research. The respondents who said they felt some pressures every workday were in the lower ranks and pay grades in the NOSC. In other words, those in the lowest levels of the hierarchical chain of command were the ones who reported experiencing more stress.

Turning to unfair treatments towards others with regard to "harassment," 78% had never perceived it and only 17% said they had experienced it from one to four times in a typical workday in the past fiscal year. Only 5% (three reservists) perceived it more than five times, and one reservist (no female) experienced it every day for the entire year. Regarding "discrimination," 90% said they never experienced it, and just 2% (one reservist) has experienced it all the time. As for "bullying," 83% never experienced it; yet, like harassment, nearly 5% (three reservists) experienced it every workday.

At this point, to corroborate trustworthiness and make sense of all the information resulting from the tabulation of the descriptive statistics, the researcher applied a statistical test. A chi-square was used to determine any differences in the manifestations of stress due to any of the forms of unfair treatment to others or any particular supervisory style. For this purpose, this writer introduced the following additional alternative hypothesis:

- Alternative Hypothesis four (H_{a4}): There is no significant statistical difference between stress and any expected variable (either: harassment, discrimination, bullying or supervisory style

By submitting this alternative hypothesis (H_{a4}) to the dissection of a chi-square, which is a standardized measure of discrepancies between our alternative hypothesis and the answers collected, the researcher got the following results under the circumstances described below:

$$\chi^2 = \Sigma \, (O_v - E_v)^2 \, / \, E_v$$

$[\Sigma$ = the sum of; O_v = Observable values, E_v = Expected values$]$

When distributing the number of all the participants (70) among the (5) options Likert in item #10, Q.02, we got the expected value of 14 for each possible response. This is considering the values from 0 to 70, where "0" meant that no one experienced stress and "70" meant that all have experienced it. In addition, the degree of freedom was four, resulting from subtracting one from the number of options in the Likert scale to establish at least one unit to compare against the variables. Finally, the critical value selected was .05, which established a 95% certainty about the outcome.

Item #10, Q.02

	0	1-2	3-4	5+	Every day	
E_v	70/5= 14	70/5= 14	70/5= 14	70/5= 14	70/5= 14	= 70
O_v	11	30	13	0	4	= 58

$$(O_v - E_v)^2 / E_v \; + \; (O_v - E_v)^2 / E_v \; + \; (O_v - E_v)^2 / E_v \; + \; (O_v - E_v)^2$$

$$/ E_v \; + \; (O_v - E_v)^2 / E_v$$

$(11 - 14)^2 / 14$	$(30 - 14)^2 / 14$	$(13 - 14)^2 / 14$	$(0 - 14)^2 / 14$	$(4 - 14)^2 / 14$
$(-3)^2 / 14$	$(16)^2 / 14$	$(-1)^2 / 14$	$(-14)^2 / 14$	$(-10)^2 / 14$
9 / 14	256 / 14	1 / 14	196 / 14	100 / 14
0.64	18.29	0.07	14	7.14

$$\Sigma = 0.64 + 18.29 + 0.07 + 14 + 7.14 = 40.14$$

Afterward, this result of 40.14 was fed into "R[58]" (the free software

programming language and software environment for statistical computing

and graphics) as follows: 1-pchisq (40.14, 4). The result was [1] 4.049247e-

08 (Online "R" at http://pbil.univ-lyon1.fr/Rweb). Therefore, since the

outcome was less than the upper-tail critical value of the chi-square

distribution (Charts #4 and #5)], the alternative hypothesis H_{a4} was accepted.

This outcome means that, aside for the chance of destiny, there is a particular circumstance generating stress at the NOSC Syracuse in Central New York other than the variables of harassment, bullying, discrimination or any supervisory style. In this sense, this researcher was inclined to consider that the stress manifested in this NOSC is related to the 79.31% lack of feedback obtained in item #11, Q.03, since this is the only criterion with relevant results in the descriptive statistical analysis.

Chart #04: Critical Values of Chi-square distribution Table (NIST/SEMATECH, 2012, p. 1.3.6.7.4.)

Upper-tail critical values of chi-square distribution
Probability less than the critical value

df	0.90 .10	0.95 .05	0.975 .025	0.99 .01	0.999 .001
1	2.706	3.841	5.024	6.635	10.828
2	4.605	5.991	7.378	9.210	13.816
3	6.251	7.815	9.348	11.345	16.266
4	7.779	9.488	11.143	13.277	18.467
5	9.236	11.070	12.833	15.086	20.515
6	10.645	12.592	14.449	16.812	22.458
7	12.017	14.067	16.013	18.475	24.322

The Chart #04 above contains the critical values of the chi-square distribution and the graphic in Chart #05 below, the significant level of the upper distribution. The significance level α is demonstrated with this graph, which shows a χ^2 distribution with three degrees of freedom for a two-sided test at significance level α = 0.05. In this sense, when test statistic is greater than the upper-tail critical value, the null hypothesis is rejected (NIST/SEMATECH, 2012, p. 1.3.6.7.4.)

Chart #05: Critical Values of Chi-square distribution –
Graphic (NIST/SEMATECH, 2012, p. 1.3.6.7.4.)

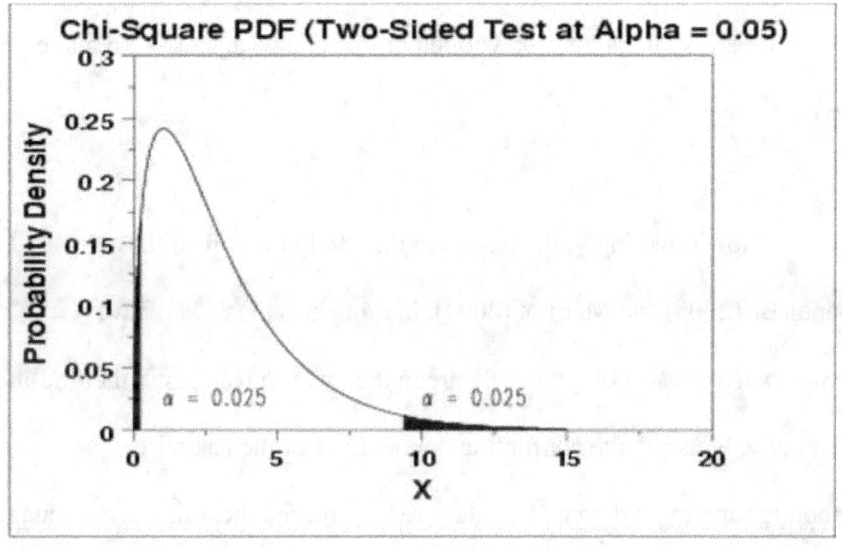

Conclusions

A factor that dramatically shaped the results of this study is the very homogenous conditions of the reservists drilling at the NOSC Syracuse in

Central New York. There is almost no diversity there, and they benefit from that quality of being very akin with respect to each other. For this reason, there were no major conflicts with respect to unfair treatments such as bullying, harassment, or discrimination. Still, 81% felt stress, even at the very low levels of one or three times in a typical workday. In contrast, 7% (four reservists) were less fortunate because they felt stress every day that year. In this regard, the most negative circumstances are those 13 reservists who felt harassed, and the six who felt discriminated against—no matter the level.

Not surprisingly, the results of this study reinforced those of Sapolsky (2005) and Marmot (2004), inasmuch as those who have experienced stress more intensely are in the lowest positions in their military hierarchy. Notably, the conflicting double lives of the reservists moonlighting in civilian and military careers placed them in a disadvantaged position. They receive constant feedback and enjoyed a more open communication about their performance in their civilian jobs for 28 days of a month. Afterward, for two days of a month during the weekends they drilled at their reserve centers or the NOSC, they confronted a shocking cultural shift in their workplace.

This dramatic change in the ambiance and climate of the workplace is undoubtedly a reflection of the armed forces' culture. In the military culture, reservists are mere pieces of the national Department of Defense, and they have a very limited voice and operate under rules, laws, and regulations that are very different from those in their civilian world. These laws are part of a different judicial system in the United States, and the ordinances are contained in the UCMJ.

Adapting is even worse for those who entered the military without prior active duty services, and this was the case for almost 24% of the reservists in the NOSC Syracuse in Central New York. Despite the circumstances, their stress levels remain relatively low. Overall, the only findings that need special attention are those cases of reservists who have experienced discrimination or harassment because that violates the policy of zero tolerance in the military.

Summary

Perhaps the real merit of this study is to have proved that there is no a statistical significant relationship between stress and the supervisory styles in place at the naval reserve training center in central New York during the military fiscal year 2013-2014. According to the results of this reseach, it is clear to this writer that the military culture plays a more important role in creating stress than the supervisory styles at the training centers for reservists or the Naval Operational Support Centers (NOSCs). Still, to discuss the possible implications of these results, it is necessary to research the terrains of the collective perceptions of their community intertwined with the memories of the social discourse of military life. Culture is, among other things, a phenomenon closely related to the conformation of the historical narrative of a nation, as well as, any organization.

Chapter V: Discussions

Possible Implications of Outcomes

To discern about military culture, one should start looking at the definition of the terms. In words of Terry Eagleton (2000) "*culture* is said to be one of the two or three most complex words in the English language" (p. 14). In his book, *The Idea of Culture,* he denoted one of the most significant changes in a masterful historical analysis of the semantics of the word. He wrote: "Culture at first denoted a thoroughly material process, which was then metaphorically transposed to affairs of the spirit. The word thus charts

within its semantic unfolding humanity's shift from rural to urban existence"
(Eagleton, 2000, p. 14).

It is amazing how the semantic rationalization of one word could make transparent the social history of its evolution. This is how the gigantic step in the transformation from an agrarian to industrial society with the modernization of the metropolis has changed the meaning of the word *culture*. Many scholars have dealt with the analysis of the introspection and the underlying meaning of this term; for example, going back to the mid-20th century, Kroeber and Kluckhom (1952) stated that culture also involves explicit or implicit forms of behavior. According to them, this behavior is obtained and transferred through the system of values inherent or associated with this term. (Kroeber & Kluckhohn, 1952, p. 181).

In the same token, David Sills (1972) stated that the connotation of the word *culture* has been enriched by the exhibits of humans' behaviors and their social interactions. By themselves, these components are not considered as the exclusive elements of the word. According to Sills, the attention should be directed to the norms, the rules of social relations, and the implicit criteria of public behavior. (Sills, 1972, p. 308). In short, the meaning of the word *culture* from a military point of view is made up of all the elements of its environment, including the traditions and values transmitted in the life of a soldier within the ranks of his or her regiment.

Military culture is the set of psychological, spiritual, and material elements shaping the identity and purpose of this community to distinguish it from many others. In a holistic way, its members are transformed and acclimatized by their interactions with each other. This way, each member is an object and a subject of the culture in which he or she is socialized. In other words, these elements shape the soldiers, who, in turn, will develop the insights that could spill over onto others with whom the soldiers maintain social interactions.

In the particular case of the military culture in the United States, one needs to recognize that the troops have a career that defines their lifestyles. Hardly any other career could have comparable demands, considering that this can demand the very life of its participants. Therefore, this creates a unique set of principles and values that affect not only a soldier, but the members of his/her families, established under the combatants' state of consciousness. For most people, a job is just what they do for living, but soldiers' jobs deeply shape and define those in their ranks.

This institutional urbanity is called *military culture* and helps to maintain "order and discipline." For such, commanders in all branches of the services have broad authority over the personal affairs of their subordinates and are personally responsible for resolving any problems that could affect the performance of their duties. For example, a commander can be notified if a soldier gets drunk, bounces a check, or has high or delayed debts. The commander is notified if a service member abuses his or her spouse or if there is any neglect of any of his or her children. In some cases, he even gets a report if a child of a service member misbehaves in school or gets in trouble with the law.

Troops on active duty need permission to leave their assigned areas, including weekends and holidays. These soldiers are subject to fulfilling ordinances at any time or day—the only thing guaranteed is eight hours of rest. They are instructed about what to wear, where to live, and who to socialize with among their fellow service members. They are told what they can and cannot put in their bodies and are informed about the restrictions on counseling services. In fact, it was not long ago that the approval of their commander was required to get married.

For the service members and their families, the "military life offers a sense of community with clearly defined rules and expectations[59]." Members of the armed forces and their families share a unique bond, professional ethics, and a sound system with rigorous values and demands. The armed forces provide a sense of community and camaraderie that is unlikely to be found in any other profession. Military culture also encourages a combative spirit that rewards strong physical and emotional skills and frowns upon weakness or humility.

Military culture, both for those on active duty or reservists, promotes the attentiveness and punctuality for the performance of duties and severely condemns delays. This culture does not accept excuses and instead denies them—no matter how reasonable they may seem. Military culture equally promotes the quiet acceptance of the orders of the superiors who do not need to provide any feedback to their subordinates. Under these guidelines, no matter how stressful it may be to execute these regulations, military personnel must closely follow the dictates of their statutes.

Limitations of Study

With regard to limitations, the writer will refer to two types. On one hand, the first is understood as the limitations in the design, covering those things that came to light, or those things that caught the attention of the researcher soon after completion of the study. On the other hand, there are circumstances, conditions, or obstacles that limited the execution of this research paper. The following two groups of limitations highlight the major challenges encountered during the completion of this research study.

Limitations in the design

The process of preparing the questionnaire included several revisions, and its pilot test was administered to a volunteer group of military servicemen. Besides all these efforts, there were some unforeseen flaws during the design process of the survey. For example, the design lacked the questioning to the reservists about their deployments' history. This question should have eliminated any potential noise from the results of those with possible cases of post-traumatic stress disorder (PTSD)[60].

With respect to the questionnaire, it is possible to predict plausible responses, yet it is still impossible to predict the real outcomes, as there will always be blame in the formulation of the questions or a lament for not asking them differently. Although there are countless ways to ask the same query, one may not formulate the appropriate Likert scale to identify the underlying conditions of a particular phenomenon. Unfortunately, during the tabulation of the study, the flaws in the selections of a Likert or question become finally evident. These issues are as important as the study itself, and the researcher must take these into account for any subsequent study. For those interested in the topic, the goal is to understand it better and avoid the same mistakes in future research whenever possible.

We will now review some of the limitations in the questionnaire and then discuss the shortcomings in the implementation of the research. Starting with the item nine, corresponding to question one, the question in the group targeting stress indicators, this did not denote clearly the precise time it was referring to in the query. It is true that the researcher explained to the different groups participating, to please, adhere to the fiscal military year starting in October 2013 and ending in September 2014. Additionally, in questions four, five, and six, it was clearly stated that the answers needed to be based on "the fiscal year ending." This should have been more precise:

"…this fiscal year ended in September 2014."

One of the participants commented that question one did not clarify

whether the change of "mood" was positive or negative, leaving the question

in doubt about the possible reaction of the interviewee. The researcher

considered this as standing out, in that when one speaks of a "change in

mood[61]," they are usually referring to a negative adjustment. Conceptually,

the term carries a negative connotation per se, and a change in mood is not a

synonym for happiness. It is also true that the query about how often one felt

happy in the workplace was not asked directly.

Moving along to other issues with the questionnaire, the set of

questions from 14 to 25 and from 27 to 31 had issues. In these two groups,

the Likert sets were the same and did not provide any discontinuity to force

analyzing, meditating, or making a distinct judgment before giving an answer

to these questions. What should have been different were the parameters in

the sets of Likert scales to avoid identical replies in the same columns and to

serve as the mechanism that prevented the basic tendency of answering and

to force the respondents to choose their answers by reasoning.

Limitations in the implementation

Initially, the study design included the Naval Operational Support

Centers (NOSC) in Buffalo, Rochester, and Syracuse in the state of New

York. However, since NOSC Rochester did not allow all the sailors to

participate openly, the five collected responses were not included to avoid

any possible bias. With the participation in the NOSC Rochester being

compromised, the researcher immediately shredded these responses. This

action eliminated any chance of mixing those responses with the others

obtained under the rigor demanded by the study.

Regarding the NOSC Buffalo, the support given by the commanding

officer and the chief was extraordinary, but the motivation to gain the sailors'

participation lacked completely. The center had too many activities taking

place when the survey was circulated in September 2014 at the end of the

naval fiscal year and this compromised the sailors' attention. Only seven

service members chose to participate at that time. Thereafter, the surveys

were sent to all the reservists drilling at the center during the next two

months. Unfortunately, the total responses collected only rose to 13. Given

that this number is not of any statistical significance, the researcher decided to shred them so as not to alter the size of the population or the sample size needed.

In the end, this research study was reduced to the NOSC Syracuse. The problem with getting the motivation and participation at the NOSC Buffalo and Rochester was mainly due to the inability of this writer to be there to administer the surveys in the same way he did at the NOSC Syracuse. In this last one, the researcher obtained the approval and was present to motivate the participants. Furthermore, this personal interaction with the members of the different units helped to clarify any possible objections to, or rejections of, the study.

As for the limitations related to the behavior of the participants, only one of the respondents decided not to take this research study seriously. First, this participant did not answer any of the demographic inquiries. As for the rest of the queries in the questionnaire, he (literally) decided to draw a line in the midpoint of all the answers. For this reason, although there were 59 participants, only 58 were officially considered. In addition, no matter the questionnaire explicitly indicated at the bottom of page one "please see reverse," two of the respondents did not realize that the survey had two pages (front and reverse sides).

More, only 58 signed consent forms were received. Therefore, survey 59, which does not have any demographics, it likely came from the person who did not sign the consent form. This questionnaire openly lacked the required stringency for this research, and for this reason, it was excluded. Still, it has been saved along with the others from NOSC Syracuse as requested by the Institutional Review Board [IRB] at SUNY Buffalo State for a lapse of three years. This action is required "to act in compliance with federal research regulations" (Amdur, Bankert, & Amdur, 2011, p. 90) and the SUNY statutory guidelines.

Finally, one of the participants mentioned that not all of the questions were related to stress according to supervisory styles (separate from demographics). He was concerned with mood changes and commented on item number 09, corresponding to question Q.01. He said that it was possible that an interviewee could have experienced mood changes (good or bad, according to him) that were entirely unrelated to the supervisory style of his or her superior. In contrast, the sole concern this writer recognized was the fact that there was not a question related to the happiness one may have felt after leaving the workplace.

Future Research

One only needs to look at the wave of soldiers coming back from foreign wars to appreciate the seriousness of the problems facing military personnel in the future. There are quandaries[62] of all kinds that affect not only active-duty combatants but also those in the reserves. Reservists are increasingly engaging in more operations and more high-level operations, given the economic constraints of the nation. This financial pressure is forcing their activation since there are no resources to keep them indefinitely doing nothing and just sitting on the benches.

The world climate seems to deteriorate more every day rather than getting better. International differences in religion, land disputes, and the high ambitions of power from some dictators do not predict any signs of peace and prosperity—quite the opposite. It is like a black cloud creating a unique environment conducive only to more wars. That is, more military activities seem to be in the forecasts for the United States of America.

Therefore, more training for soldiers will be needed in academies and RTCs, as well as in the NOSCs.

In such a way, the ultimate cure for soldiers returning from the battlefield with health problems will not be in the hospitals. They will need long hours of therapy to overcome the trauma and to recover from both, physical and mental illnesses. However, for those in the reserves who are in constant training; why not make their lives more enjoyable by trying to reduce the stress level in the reserve centers where they are drilling.

In order to do this, it is necessary to conduct further studies on the conditions that may be affecting the reserves in their workplaces. It is important to determine the best means of defense in the battlefields, and similarly, it is fundamentally necessary to determine the finest training possible and the appropriate ambiance at the reserve centers. National studies should be the best practice for determining what is creating stress in the workplace. This process is necessary in order to eliminate what is not contributing to the better quality of the reservists' training.

Ideally, the best procedure would be to conduct a comparative study of the private companies where the reservists work. Since they have authorized moonlight jobs, it would be important to see if there are any spillovers from their civilian lives into their military lives or vice versa. These studies should be channeled through the Department of Defense. This institution, in turn, should open the doors to the national focal points of the NOSC for such studies to have the needed support to ensure the appropriate statistical size for the research. Moreover, studies can be extended to reservists in all branches of the armed forces in the United States.

An awareness campaign would also help soldiers become more cooperative in relation to studies on their behalf. There should not be long and detailed explanations about how these researches will benefit future generations. These studies should be part of the training they receive routinely since a research can be difficult for the participants to accept. The point is not only to get permission for the studies; but, once these are obtained, to motivate the target audience and get them to participate.

Regrettably, this selfless cooperation sometimes requires a pray for a miracle. In many cases, one must has to swim upstream in order to contribute to a noble cause. It is ironic that scholars have to beg to get access to studies that are obviously necessary. Military institutions should welcome any effort in the fight against stress instead. Prevention has been, and should remain, the best weapon to combat the conditions that latently may affect the optimum conditions of human life—in this case, the conditions at the reserve centers for those soldiers in the armed reserves.

References

Amdur, R. J., Bankert, E. A., & Amdur, R. J. (2011). *Institutional review board : member handbook* (3rd ed.). Sudbury, Mass.: Jones and Bartlett Publishers.

Asgar, J., & Hoffman, F. (1989). *The organizational role of supervisors* (1st ed.). Calabasas, CA: Practical Management.

Bankert, E. A., Amdur, R. J., & Amdur, R. J. (2006). *Institutional review board : management and function* (2nd ed.). Sudbury, Mass.: Jones and Bartlett.

Bekkers, V., & Homburg, V. (2002). Administrative Supervision and Information Relationships. *Information Polity, 7*(2-3), 129-141.

Britt, T. W., Adler, A. B., & Castro, C. A. (2006). *Military life : the psychology of serving in peace and combat*. Westport, Conn.: Praeger Security International.

Buelens, M., & Broeck, H. V. (2007). An Analysis of Differences in Work Motivation between Public and Private Sector Organizations. *Public Administration Review, 67*(1), 65–74. doi: 10.1111/j.1540-6210.2006.00697.x

Byrne, E. M. (1981). *Military law* (3rd ed.). Annapolis, Md.: Naval Institute Press.

Eagleton, T. (2000). *The idea of culture*. Malden, MA: Blackwell.

Eley, A. R., & Murray, R. (2009). *How to be an Effective Supervisor: Best practice in research student supervision*. Maidenhead ; New York: Open University Press.

Fehr, G. P. (2010). *The Unwritten Rules: Leadership in the Work Place* Bloomington, IN: AuthorHouse.

Fernando, D. M., & Hulse-Killacky, D. (2005). The Relationship of Supervisory Styles to Satisfaction With Supervision and the Perceived Self-Efficacy of Master's-Level Counseling Students. *Counselor Education & Supervision, Volume 44*(Issue 4), 293-304. doi: 10.1002/j.1556-6978.2005.tb01757.x

Foege, W. H. (2005). *Global health leadership and management* (1st ed.). San Francisco: Jossey-Bass.

Garfield, E. (1981). Introducing Discover. *Time Inc.'s Monthly Magazine of Science, Vol. 5,* 52-56.

Gatfield, T. (2005). An Investigation into PhD Supervisory Management Styles: Development of a dynamic conceptual model and its managerial implications. *Journal of Higher Education Policy and Management, Vol. 27*(Iss. 3), 311-325. doi: 10.1080/13600800500283585

Green, S. G., & Krasikova, D. V. (2013). Destructive leadership: a theoretical review, integration, and future research agenda. *Journal of management, 39*(5), 1308-1338. doi: 10.1177/0149206312471388

Henry, N. (2013). *Public administration and public affairs* (12th ed.). Boston: Pearson.

Herz, R. P., & Wolf, M. B. (2010). *Human factors issues in combat identification*. Farnham, Surrey, England ; Burlington, VT: Ashgate.

Jefferies, C. L. (1977). Public Administration and the Military. *Public Administration Review, 37*(No. 4 (Jul. - Aug., 1977)), pp. 321-333.

Johnson, S., & Doyle, M. L. (2010). *I'm still standing : from captive U.S. soldier to free citizen-- my journey home* (1st Touchstone hardcover ed.). New York: Simon & Schuster.

Karney, B. R., & Crown, J. S. (2007). *Families under stress : an assessment of data, theory, and reseach on marriage and divorce in the military*. Santa Monica, CA: RAND Corp.

Kottler, J. A., & Chen, D. D. (2011). *Stress management and prevention : applications to everyday life* (2nd ed.). New York, NY: Routledge.

Kroeber, A. L., & Kluckhohn, C. (1952). *Culture; a critical review of concepts and definitions*. Cambridge, Mass.,: The Museum.

Leigh, J. P. (2000). *Costs of occupational injuries and illnesses*. Ann Arbor: University of Michigan Press.

Lovallo, W. R. (2005). *Stress & health : biological and psychological interactions* (2nd ed.). Thousand Oaks, Calif.: Sage Publications.

Mannitz, S. (2012). *Democratic civil-military relations : soldiering in 21st-century Europe*. London ; New York: Routledge.

Marmot, M. (2006). *Why care? : how status affects our health and longevity*. New York, NY: International Longevity Center-USA.

Marmot, M. G. (2004). *The status syndrome : how social standing affects our health and longevity* (1st American ed.). New York: Times Books.

National_Geography (Producer). (2008). Stress: portrait of a killer. [DVD] Retrieved from http://topdocumentaryfilms.com/stress-portrait-of-a-killer

NIST/SEMATECH. (2012). e-Handbook of Statistical Methods. Retrieved 11-27-14, from http://www.itl.nist.gov/div898/handbook/index.htm

Prociuk, T. J., Breen, L. J., & Lussier, R. J. (1976). Hopelessness, internal-external locus of control, and depression. *Journal of Clinical Psychology, Volume 32,* 299–300.

Ramchand, R., & Center for Military Health Policy Research. (2011). *The war within : preventing suicide in the U.S. military*. Santa Monica, CA: Rand Corporation.

Ravasi, D., & Schultz, M. (2006). Exploring the role of organizational culture. *Academy of Management Journal, 49* 433–458.

Reid, C. (2009). *The Wounds of Exclusion: Poverty, Women's Health, and Social Justice* Walnut Creek, California: Left Coast Press.

Rogers, C. (2008). *Leadership skills in policing*. Oxford ; New York: Oxford University Press.

Sapolsky, M. (2002). *A primate's memoir: a neuroscientist's unconventional life among the baboons* (Reprint edition ed.). New York: Scribner.

Shulman, L. (2010). *Interactional supervision* (3rd ed.). Washington, DC: NASW Press.

Sills, D. L. (1972). *International encyclopedia of the social sciences* (Reprint ed.). New York: Macmillan Co. & The Free Press.

Tick, E. (2014). *Warrior's return : restoring the soul after war*.

United States. Office of the Chief Army Reserve. Army reservist. Washington,: U.S. Office of the Chief.

Uradnik, K. A., Johnson, L. A., & Hower, S. (2011). *Battleground : government and politics*. Santa Barbara, Calif.: Greenwood.

WHO. (n.d.). Stress at the workplace.   Retrieved November 30, 2014, from http://www.who.int/occupational_health/topics/stressatwp/en

Wofford, M. (2012). *Make difficult people disappear : how to deal with stressful behavior and eliminate conflict*. Hoboken, N.J.: Wiley.

Zimbardo, P. G. (1985). *Psychology and life* (11th ed.). Glenview, Ill.: Scott, Foresman.

Endnotes

[1] B.Ed. UASD/DWU Dominican Republic, Certification in Human Resources UPID Dominican Republic, MS Finances UNAM Mexico D.F., BS Business & Economics SUNY ESC, MA Spanish Linguistics/Literature SUNY at UB, CLSSGB SUNY at UB, MPA Public Administration SUNY at Buffalo State.

[2] Stress: In psychology, a state of bodily or mental tension resulting from factors that tend to alter an existent equilibrium. Stress is an unavoidable effect of living and is an especially complex phenomenon in modern technological society. It has been linked to coronary heart disease, psychosomatic disorders, and various other mental and physical problems. Treatment usually consists of a combination of counseling or psychotherapy and medication. See "stress." (2009). Encyclopædia Britannica 2009 Ready Reference. Chicago: Encyclopædia Britannica.

[3] Descriptive Statistics: Descriptive statistics is concerned with the tabulation and classification of data, graphical representation, and the calculation of certain summarizing values to describe group characteristics of the particular data. Analytical statistics deals with the plans for taking observations, the analysis of these data, and the drawing of inferences from them. See "Statistics" Bancroft, T. A. (2014). Statistics. Encyclopedia Americana. Retrieved October 1, 2014, from Grolier Online http://ea.grolier.com/article?id=0368810-00

[4] Supervision: It might be obvious that supervisors are people in an organization who have subordinates working for them, and that we have supervisors who make sure that work is done as effectively as possible. However, as we begin to define the job of a supervisor, it becomes clear that the job is much more significant than just having others working for a supervisor, especially when we start considering a supervisor on the management team. See Asgar, J., & Hoffman, F. (1989). The organizational role of supervisors (1st ed.). Calabasas, CA: Practical Management.

[5] Supervisory Styles: A number of studies have been done of supervisory style with general agreement that a relatively good match between student and supervisor in preferred style is supportive of a productive relationship. The studies also indicate that the notion of an appropriate style changes, depending on the context, the stage the student has reached and the individual research students involved. For instance, one study (Gatfield, 2005) developed a model of supervisory styles by reviewing

the literature. Then in order to assess the value of the model, he examined the preferred styles of supervisors who had been designated as excellent by their Dean (high completion rates within the normally expected time frame, multiple supervisions, and excellent supervisory reports). They were interviewed and asked to place themselves within one of four quadrants, representing different styles: pastoral, contractual, laissez-faire, and directorial. While three-quarters chose the Contractual Style quadrant (high structure and support), more important was the finding that these excellent supervisors made a transition from one style to the other during candidature, in the main when the candidate a) was in crisis; and b) made a transition through various stages. In other words, they recognized that each supervisory relationship is unique, requiring different skills and approaches. See Supervisory styles, OLI. (n.d.). Retrieved from https://www.learning.ox.ac.uk/ supervision/supervisor/styles

[6] De Facto: a Latin term meaning "in fact" or "actually," is often applied in the context of corporation law and international law. See "De facto" Weinstein, P. D. (2014). De Facto. *Encyclopedia Americana.* Retrieved October 1, 2014, from Grolier Online http://ea.grolier.com/article?id=0122250-00

[7] Somatic: "Do you ever have strange, unexplained feelings in your body? Many people do, such as a sudden pain in the head or a twinge in the abdomen. Most of us pay little attention to these changes because they are not severe and do not last long" (Kearney & Trull, 2011 p. 158). Kearney, C. A., & Trull, T. J. (2011). Abnormal psychology and life: A dimensional approach. Belmont, CA: Wadsworth Pub Co.

[8] Labour instead of labor to emphasized the physical activity linked to military activities.

Labour: productive work, esp physical toil done for wages. The people, class, or workers involved in this, esp in contrast to management, capital, etc. (as modifier): a labour dispute, labour relations. See "labour." (n.d.). Dictionary.com Unabridged. Retrieved October 1, 2014, from Dictionary.com website: http://dictionary.reference.com/browse/labour

[9] Ancillaries: a subsidiary or auxiliary thing or person: the company has an ancillary abroad. See "Ancillary." (n.d.). Dictionary.com Unabridged. Retrieved October 01, 2014, from Dictionary.com website: http://dictionary.reference.com/browse/ancillary

[10] U.S. Department of Defense. (n.d.). Retrieved from http://www.defense.gov/pubs/ Mobilization-Weekly-Report-141125.pdf

[11] Rank: Military rank is the system of titles that forms the hierarchy of the armed services. […] The first title to acquire general currency was that of admiral, which was derived from the Arabic amir-al-bahr, "prince of the sea," by which the leader of the Muslim fleet in the Mediterranean was known as early as the 12th century. The term was brought back to Europe by the Crusaders, who spelled it by analogy with the Latin admirabilis, "admirable." As late as the 16th century, however, the word was applied as often to the commander's ship as to the man, who was more often called general, […] captain general. […]During the 19th century the extra rank of lieutenant commander was invented to distinguish senior lieutenants in larger ships. These additions recognized that the steam navy required [a] considerable hierarchy of officers to perform a variety of functions unknown in simple sailing-ship days. See "Rank" Keegan, J. (2014). Rank, Military. Grolier Multimedia Encyclopedia. Retrieved October 2, 2014, from Grolier Online http://gme.grolier.com/article?assetid=0242495-0

[12] RTC: Recruit Training Command Great Lakes (Naval Station Great Lakes), is a unit within the United States Navy primarily responsible for conducting the initial orientation and indoctrination of incoming recruits. "The training command provides basic naval training and advanced training in various technical schools. Leading Chicago merchants bought the land in 1905 and gave it to the government. The Navy commissioned the station in 1911." See "Naval Station Great Lakes" Reid, W. W. (2014). Naval Station Great Lakes. In Public Libraries. Retrieved from http://www.worldbookonline.com/pl/infofinder/article?id=ar234280

[13] Squalor: very bad and dirty conditions. The quality or state of being Squalid. Latin *squalidus* rough, dirty, from *squalēre* to be covered with scales or dirt, from *squalus* dirty; perhaps akin to Latin*squama* scale. See "Squalor" Squalor. (n.d.) Retrieved October 2, 2014, from http://www.merriam-webster.com/dictionary/squalor.

[14] MOS: For enlisted members of the Armed Services, professional education begins with basic training, or boot camp, followed by advanced technical training in one of the many occupational and vocational fields required by increasingly complex and technologically advanced organizations. Members receive a Military Occupational Specialty (MOS) designation upon successful completion of this training. The military-skill training component of precommissioning programs has much in common with basic training. Following an initial tour of duty, selected Army enlisted members attend the NCOES Basic Course, which focuses on small-unit

leadership. See "M.O.S." CAINE, BRUCE T. "Military Professional Education System." Encyclopedia of Education. Ed. James W. Guthrie. 2nd ed. Vol. 5. New York: Macmillan Reference USA, 2002. 1653-1655. Gale Virtual Reference Library. Web. 2 Dec. 2014.

[15] AT: Selected Reserve of SELRES personnel must perform 12 to 14 days AT/ADT each fiscal year as scheduled by the unit CO and per COMNAVRESFORCOM's annual Fiscal Year Policy Execution Guidance notice. Waivers of the AT requirement (section 1305) may be authorized under the direction of COMNAVRESFORCOM. Failure to perform AT or obtain a waiver will result in unsatisfactory participation for the fiscal year (see chapter 11, section 1106). AT that overlaps 2 fiscal years may be considered as satisfying the requirement for either fiscal year; however, retirement point credit will be applied only to the anniversary year in which it was earned. Members of the IRR are not entitled to perform AT. See "AT" Administrative Procedures for Navy Reservists - BUPERSINST 1001.39F - PERS-9 from Bureau of Naval Personnel at the Department of the Navy. Retrieved from http://www.public.navy.mil/bupers-npc/reference/instructions/BUPERSInstructions/Documents/1001.39F.pdf

[16] UCMJ: Uniform Code of Military Justice replaced the traditional system known as the Articles of War, which governed the conduct of military personnel from 1775 to the UCMJ's passage in 1950. The Articles of War contained eighteenth-century language inappropriate to the post–World War II military and contained separate legal systems for the army and navy. The UCMJ was a product of the newly created Office of the Secretary of Defense, which centralized and regularized many facets of military life. The UCMJ was written entirely by civilians, with first Secretary of Defense James Forrestal (1947-1949) making many of the key decisions himself. In many of its aspects, the UCMJ is significantly more restrictive than civilian law. See "UCMJ" Byrne, Edward. Military Law: A Handbook for the Navy and Marine Corps. Annapolis, Md.: Naval Institute Press, 1981.

[17] W.H.O.: Public-health agency of the UN, established in Geneva in 1948 to succeed two earlier agencies. Its mandate is to promote "the highest possible level of health" in all peoples. Its work falls into three categories. It provides a clearinghouse for information on the latest developments in disease and health care and establishes international sanitary standards and quarantine measures. It sponsors measures for the control of epidemic and endemic disease (including immunization campaigns and assistance in providing sources of pure water). Finally, it encourages the strengthening of public-

health programs in member nations. Its greatest success to date has been the worldwide eradication of smallpox (1980). See "World Health Organization (W.H.O.)."   (2009). *Encyclopædia Britannica 2009 Ready Reference. Chicago*: Encyclopædia Britannica.

[18] American Institute of Stress, The: A.I.S. is a non-profit organization which imparts information on stress reduction, stress in the workplace, effects of stress and various other stress related topics. A.I.S. was founded in 1978, at the request of Dr. Hans Selye to serve as a clearinghouse of all stress related information. Today, AIS provides a diverse and inclusive environment that fosters intellectual discovery creates and transmits innovative knowledge, improves human health and provides leadership to the world on stress related topics.
see "American Institute of Stress" dedicated to advancing the understanding of Stress in Health and Illness. (n.d.). Retrieved from http://www.stress.org

[19] Depression: Neurotic or psychotic disorder marked by sadness, inactivity, difficulty in thinking and concentration, a significant increase or decrease in appetite and time spent sleeping, feelings of rejection and hopelessness, and sometimes suicidal tendencies. Probably the most common psychiatric complaint, depression has been described by physicians from at least the time of Hippocrates, who called it melancholia. Its course is extremely variable from person to person; it may be fleeting or permanent, mild or severe. Depression is more common in women than in men. The rates of incidence increase with age in men, while the peak for women is between the ages of 35 and 45. Its causes can be both psychosocial and biochemical. Treatment is usually a combination of psychotherapy and drug therapy. See "depression." (2009). Encyclopædia Britannica 2009 Ready Reference. Chicago: Encyclopædia Britannica.

[20] Psychosomatic disorders: Bodily ailment or symptom, caused by mental or emotional disturbance, in which psychological stresses adversely affect physiological (somatic) functioning to the point of distress. Psychosomatic disorders may include hypertension, respiratory ailments, gastrointestinal disturbances, migraine and tension headaches, sexual dysfunctions, and dermatitis. Many patients with psychosomatic conditions respond to a combination of drug therapy and psychotherapy. See "psychosomatic disorders." (2009). Encyclopædia Britannica 2009 Ready Reference. Chicago: Encyclopædia Britannica.

[21] Ambiance: "perhaps the main driving force of Workplace Health Promotion (WHP), is a concept already enshrined in human resources'

planning: investing in something that will improve the whole atmosphere in the workplace is attractive to human resources, and many programs are implemented with this purpose. When employees acknowledge that they are taken care of, they commit themselves much more to the company and to the employer" (Kirsten & Karch, 2012, p. 52). Kirsten, W., & Karch, R. C. (2012). Global perspectives in workplace health promotion. Sudbury, MA: Jones & Bartlett Learning.

[22] Jurisprudence: Science or philosophy of law. Jurisprudence may be divided into three branches: analytical, sociological, and theoretical. The analytical branch articulates axioms, defines terms, and prescribes the methods that best enable one to view the legal order as an internally consistent, logical system. The sociological branch examines the actual effects of the law within society and the influence of social phenomena on the substantive and procedural aspects of law. The theoretical branch evaluates and criticizes law in terms of the ideals or goals postulated for it. See "jurisprudence." (2009). Encyclopædia Britannica 2009 Ready Reference. Chicago: Encyclopædia Britannica.

[23] Coronary: of or relating to the heart and especially to the vessels that supply blood to the heart. See "Coronary." (n.d.) Retrieved November 12, 2014, from http://www.merriam-webster.com/dictionary/coronary.

[24] Per se: by, of, or in itself : by, of, or in itself or oneself or themselves : as such : intrinsically : being such inherently, clearly, or as a matter of law <a per se conflict of interest> See "Per se." (n.d.). Retrieved November 12, 2014, from http://www.merriam-webster.com/dictionary/per se.

[25] Bellicose: warlike; aggressive; ready to fight : from Latin bellicōsus, from bellum war. Synonyms: aggressive, offensive, hostile, destructive, defiant, provocative, belligerent, combative, antagonistic, pugnacious, hawkish, warlike, quarrelsome, militaristic, sabre-rattling, jingoistic, warmongering, aggers (Australian, slang) • bellicose statements threatening tough action. See "bellicose." (n.d.). Collinsdictionary.com. Retrieved November 23, 2014, from Collinsdictionary.com website: http://www.collinsdictionary.com/dictionary/english-thesaurus /bellicose?showCookiePolicy=true

[26] Hybrid: a person whose background is a blend of two diverse cultures or traditions : an animal or plant that is produced from two animals or plants of different kinds : something that is formed by combining two or more things : an offspring of two animals or plants of different races, breeds,

varieties, species, or genera : something heterogeneous in origin or composition : composite <hybrids of complementary DNA and RNA strands> <a hybrid of medieval and Renaissance styles> : something (as a power plant, vehicle, or electronic circuit) that has two different types of components performing essentially the same function See "Hybrid." (n.d.). Retrieved November 22, 2014, from http://www.merriam-webster.com/dictionary/hybrid.

[27] Treatise: (noun), a written work dealing formally and systematically with a subject. "a comprehensive treatise on electricity and magnetism" synonyms: disquisition, essay, paper, work, exposition, discourse, dissertation, thesis, monograph, opus, oeuvre, study, critique, tract, pamphlet, account. See "treatise. (n.d.). *Dictionary.com Unabridged.* Retrieved November 21, 2014, from Dictionary.com website: http://dictionary.reference.com/browse/treatise.

[28] Moonlight: "Why do workers in the United States and Canada moonlight? The evidence cited so far shows that there are many reasons, reflecting many factors, including age, education, marital status, and household composition. As explained by Conway and Kimmel (1998), the reasons for multiple-job holding can be summarized as constraints on the primary job (insufficient hours or earnings) or heterogeneous jobs (different jobs provide different nonpecuniary benefits to the worker.) These sorts of reasons for moonlighting can he identified in both the Canadian and U.S. data sources because individual workers report specific reasons [...] for taking a second job" (Wong & Picot, 2001 p. 310). Wong, G., & Picot, W. G. (2001). Working time in comparative perspective. Kalamazoo, MI: W.E. Upjohn Institute for Employment Research.

[29] Social Status: Status refers to a person's position within an institutional or organizational framework. Thus, being middle class is a general status position within the system of social stratification. Status is the positional element in a structure or organization; role refers to the behavior associated with status. Both status and role can be reduced to the characterizations and behavioral expectations that constitute the foundation of all social life. Sociologist Talcott Parsons, for example, made what he called the "status role bundle" his basic analytical unit. The concept of status group (or "social class," a virtual synonym) has been of great importance for sociological studies of communities. Early studies, such as those of W. Lloyd Warner and Paul S. Lunt, regarded the status systems of the American community as fundamental aspects of their structure. Warner

suggested the model of a community as a kind of layer cake of status groups (or social classes), based on his study of Newburyport, Mass.; a whole generation of community sociologists employed his model. See Westby, D. (2014). "Status." Grolier Multimedia Encyclopedia. Retrieved November 12, 2014, from Grolier Online http://gme.grolier.com/article?assetid=0275905-0

[30] Mesmeric: of, relating to, or induced by mesmerism : fascinating, irresistible. See "Mesmeric." (n.d.). Retrieved November 22, 2014, from http://www.merriam-webster.com/dictionary/mesmeric

[31] Baboon: Any of five species of robust monkeys (Genus Papio) of Arabia and sub-Saharan Africa. Baboons have a large head, cheek pouches, and a long, doglike muzzle. They walk on all fours, carrying the tail in a characteristic arch. They weigh 30–90 lbs (14–40 kg) and are about 20–45 in. (50–115 cm) long, excluding the tail (18–28 in., or 45–70 cm, long). Found mainly in drier savanna and rocky areas, they feed on a variety of plants and animals. Highly social and intelligent, they travel in large noisy troops, communicating by calls. They may destroy crops, and their enormous canine teeth and powerful limbs make them dangerous opponents. See "baboon.: (2009). Encyclopædia Britannica 2009 Ready Reference. Chicago: Encyclopædia Britannica.

[32] Cortisol: "(hydrocortisone) is the major glucocorticoid produced and secreted by the adrenal cortex. It affects the metabolism of protein, fat, and carbohydrates; maintenance of muscle and myocardial integrity; and the suppression of inflammatory and allergic activities" (Williamson & Snyder, 2015, p. 1200). Williamson, M. A., & Snyder, L. M. (2015). Wallach's interpretation of diagnostic tests: Pathways to arriving at a clinical diagnosis.

[33] Alpha male: "Alpha is the first letter of the Greek alphabet. In English, it has come to denote "the First of anything." In astronomy, for instance, alpha is the brightest star in a constellation. Animal researchers use the word to signify dominance, applying it to the leader of the pack, who is first in power and importance. That usage has been extended to human beings. An alpha is defined as "a person tending to assume a dominant role in social or professional situations, or thought to possess the qualities and confidence for leadership."[1] As we use the term in our work, alpha signifies a powerful, authoritative personality type with a specific set of traits. Alphas are aggressive, results-driven achievers who insist on top performance from themselves and others" (Ludeman & Erlandson, 2006, p. 2-3). Ludeman, K., & Erlandson, E. (2006). Alpha male syndrome. Boston, MA: Harvard Business School Press.

[34] Whitehall: Whitehall Palace was a group of buildings designated by the English king Henry VIII (r. 1509–47) as the premier royal residence in London. Although building on the site began in 1532, most of the work actually carried out involved only remodeling and refitting until 1619, when the architect Inigo Jones began the construction of the Banqueting House (completed 1622). This building, designed in a Renaissance style, stimulated plans by Charles I (1647) and Charles II (1661) to establish a larger palace that would cover an area from Charing Cross to Westminster. All work in progress, including Sir Christopher Wren's group of rooms south of the Banqueting House, was destroyed by fire in 1698. No attempt was made to rebuild the palace, and the whole site is now covered by a maze of government buildings, including the residence of the prime minister, 10 Downing Street (1680, rebuilt c.1723 and 1766). See Cast, D. (2014). "Whitehall Palace." Grolier Multimedia Encyclopedia. Retrieved November 12, 2014, from Grolier Online http://gme.grolier.com/article?assetid=0311700-0

[35] Social services: Any of various professional activities or methods concerned with providing social services (such as investigatory and treatment services or material aid) to disadvantaged, distressed, or vulnerable persons or groups. The field originated in the charity organizations in Europe and the U.S. in the late 19th century. The training of volunteer workers by these organizations led directly to the founding of the first schools of social work and indirectly to increased government responsibility for the welfare of the disadvantaged. Social service providers may serve the needs of children and families, the poor or homeless, immigrants, veterans, the mentally ill, the handicapped, victims of rape or domestic violence, and persons dependent on alcohol or drugs. See welfare. See "social service." (2009). Encyclopædia Britannica 2009 Ready Reference. Chicago: Encyclopædia Britannica.

[36] Billet: an official order directing that a member of a military force be provided with board and lodging (as in a private home) : quarters assigned by or as if by a billet. See "Billet." (n.d.). Retrieved November 22, 2014, from http://www.merriam-webster.com/dictionary/billet.

In the military jargon one refers to a hard billet when the order is confirmed as a permanent position for a soldier for a specified period established on it.

[37] Gene: Unit of heredity that occupies a fixed position on a chromosome. Genes achieve their effects by directing protein synthesis. They are composed of DNA, except in some viruses that contain RNA instead. The

sequence of nitrogenous bases along a strand of DNA determines the genetic code. When the product of a particular gene is needed, the portion of the DNA molecule that contains that gene splits, and a complementary strand of RNA, called messenger RNA (mRNA), forms and then passes to ribosomes, where proteins are synthesized. A second type of RNA, transfer RNA (tRNA), matches up the mRNA with specific amino acids, which combine in series to form polypeptide chains, the building blocks of proteins. Experiments have shown that many of the genes within a cell are inactive much or even all of the time, but they can be switched on and off. Mutations occur when the number or order of bases in a gene is disrupted. See genetic engineering, genetics, Hardy-Weinberg law, Human Genome Project, linkage group. See "gene." (2009). Encyclopædia Britannica 2009 Ready Reference. Chicago: Encyclopædia Britannica.

[38] Equanimity: The quality of being calm and even-tempered; composure : calmness of mind or temper; composure : composure, esp. under tension or strain; evenness of temper.
See "Equanimity." (n.d.) The American Heritage® Dictionary of the English Language, Fourth Edition. (2003). Retrieved November 22 2014 from http://www.thefreedictionary.com/ equanimity

[39] Per Contra: on the contrary : by way of contrast : as an offset. See "Per contra." (n.d.). Retrieved December 2, 2014, from http://www.merriam-webster.com/dictionary/per contra.

[40] Discover magazine: it reports captivating developments in science, medicine, technology, and the world around us. Spectacular photography and refreshingly understandable stories on complex subjects connect everyday people with the greatest ideas and minds in science. See "Discover." About Discover Magazine | DiscoverMagazine.com. (n.d.). Retrieved from http://discovermagazine.com/magazine/about/2012/10/about-discover-magazine.

The monthly magazine was launched in October 1980 by Time Inc. It was sold to Family Media, the owners of Health, in 1987. The Walt Disney Company bought the magazine when Family Media went out of business in 1991. In October 2005 Discover was sold to two media investment companies, and later re-sold to Kalmbach Publishing in 2010. See Eugene Garfield, "Introducing Discover", Essays of an Information Scientist, Vol:5, 16 March 1981, p.52-56

[41] Hopelessness (Hopeless thinking): it is one of the most ominous symptoms of severe depression. A number of studies have found that

hopelessness is strongly associated with suicide risk (A.T. Beck et al. 1975, 1985; Fawcett et al. 1987). For example, an investigation by A.T. Beck et al. (1975) discovered that the overall level of depressive symptoms, as measured by the Beck Depression Inventory (A.T. Beck et al. 1961), was less predictive of suicide risk than scores on the Beck hopelessness Scale (BHS; A.T. Beck et al. 1974). Another study found that elevated BHS values on discharge from a psychiatric hospital were the strongest predictor of risk for future suicide (A.T. Beck et al. 1985). See "Hopelessness" Wright, J. H. (2009, p.146). Cognitive-behavior therapy for severe mental illness: An illustrated guide. Washington, DC: American Psychiatric Pub.

[42] Locus of control: This is a psychological concept that refers to how strongly people believe they have control over the situations and experiences that affect their lives. In education, locus of control typically refers to how students perceive the causes of their academic success or failure in school. See "Locus of Control" Definition - The Glossary of Education Reform. (n.d.). Retrieved from http://edglossary.org/locus-of-control

[43] The Global Health Council is a United States-based non-profit networking organizing linking "several hundred health non-governmental organizations (NGOs) around the world to share knowledge and resources, build partnerships and together become stronger advocates for health". The Council is the world's largest membership alliance dedicated to advancing policies and programs that improve health around the world. See Foege, William H.; Nils Daulaire; Robert E. Black; Clarence E. Pearson (2005). Global Health Leadership and Management: partners in global health and development. San Francisco: Jossey-Bass. ISBN 9780787971533. Retrieved 2008-10-22.

[44] National Geographic: U.S. scientific society founded in 1888 in Washington, D.C., by a small group of eminent explorers and scientists "for the increase and diffusion of geographic knowledge." At the turn of the 21st century it had approximately nine million members. It has supported more than 7,000 major scientific projects and expeditions, including those of Robert E. Peary, Richard E. Byrd, the Leakey family, Jacques-Yves Cousteau, Jane Goodall, and Dian Fossey. It has published numerous books, atlases, and bulletins and has created hundreds of television documentaries. National Geographic Magazine is a monthly magazine of geography, archaeology, anthropology, and exploration. It became a leader in reproducing colour photographs and printing photographs of undersea life,

views from the stratosphere, and animals in their natural habitats. It also became famous for articles containing substantial information on environmental, social, and cultural aspects of the regions covered. See Gilbert Grosvenor. See "National Geographic Society." (2009). Encyclopædia Britannica 2009 Ready Reference. Chicago: Encyclopædia Britannica.

[45] Homo sapiens: Latin "wise man." Species to which all modern human beings belong. The oldest known fossil remains date to c. 120,000 years ago—or much earlier (c. 400,000 years ago) if evidence of certain archaic varieties is included. Homo sapiens is distinguished from earlier hominin species by characteristics and habits such as bipedal stance and gait, brain capacity averaging about 1,350 cc, high forehead, small teeth and jaw, defined chin, construction and use of tools, and ability to use symbols. Most scholars believe that modern humans developed in Africa c. 150,000 years ago and spread to the Middle East c. 100,000 years ago and to other parts of Eurasia c. 40,000–50,000 years ago (this is known as the "single-origin" model). Others contend that modern humans developed from various regional populations of archaic H. sapiens or even other species of Homo in Eurasia beginning c. 250,000 years ago (the "multiregional" model). In the first model the genetic differences that exist between the peoples of the world would not be very old; in the second model they would be significantly older. In any case, by c. 11,000 BC modern H. sapiens had peopled virtually the entire globe. See Cro-Magnon; culture; human evolution; Neanderthal. See "Homo sapiens" (2009). Encyclopædia Britannica 2009 Ready Reference. Chicago: Encyclopædia Britannica.

[46] Industrial Revolution: Process of change from an agrarian, handicraft economy to one dominated by industry and machine manufacture. It began in England in the 18th century. [...] The Industrial Revolution was largely confined to Britain from 1760 to 1830 and then spread to other European nations; but, once Germany, the U.S., and Japan achieved industrial power, they outstripped Britain's initial successes. [...] Not until the mid-20th century did the Industrial Revolution spread to such countries as China and India. Industrialization effected changes in economic, political, and social organization. These included a wider distribution of wealth and increased international trade; political changes resulting from the shift in economic power; sweeping social changes that included the rise of working-class movements, the development of managerial hierarchies to oversee the division of labour, and the emergence of new patterns of authority. See

"Industrial Revolution." (2009). Encyclopædia Britannica 2009 Ready Reference. Chicago: Encyclopædia Britannica.

[47] Subaltern: Lower in position or rank; secondary : Chiefly British Holding a military rank just below that of captain : Logic In the relation of a particular proposition to a universal with the same subject, predicate, and quality. See "subaltern." (n.d.) The American Heritage® Dictionary of the English Language, Fourth Edition. (2003). Retrieved December 2 2014 from http://www.thefreedictionary.com/Subalterns.

[48] W-L-B: The scarcity perspective (involvement in multiple areas reduces the time and resources to focus on each), and personality integration (those high on the personality traits experience less stress and work-life conflict, while they are more competent performing in each position) (Rykr, 2009). See Rykr, E. (2009). "The Work-Life-Balance Concept." Available at: http://www.brazencareerist.com /2009/02/21/the-worklife-balance-concept.

[49] Social anxiety disorder: Also known as social phobia, is an intense, long-lasting fear of embarrassment in social situations. It is different from shyness or stage fright, however. Social anxiety disorder involves extreme anxiety, an unpleasant feeling of fear, worry, or nervousness. It may cause people to avoid social situations, or to feel intensely self-conscious or uncomfortable and may lead to problems at home, work, or school. See "Social Anxiety Disorder." *Complete Human Diseases and Conditions*. Ed. Neil Izenberg and Steven A. Dowshen. Vol. 3. Detroit: Charles Scribner's Sons, 2008. *Gale Virtual Reference Library*. Web. 22 Nov. 2014.

[50] Psychosocial: This term refers to the psychological and social factors that influence mental health. Social influences such as peer pressure, parental support, cultural and religious background, socioeconomic status, and interpersonal relationships all help to shape personality and influence psychological makeup. Children and adolescents with psychosocial disorders frequently have difficulty functioning in social situations and may have problems effectively communicating with others. See Ford-Martin, Paula. "Psychosocial Personality Disorders." The Gale Encyclopedia of Children's Health: Infancy through Adolescence. Ed. Kristine Krapp and Jeffrey Wilson. Vol. 3. Detroit: Gale, 2006. 1532-1535. Gale Virtual Reference Library. Web. 22 Nov. 2014.

[51] Bullying: "The confusion inherent in the definition of bullying makes it challenging to address and intervene[3]. Very simply, if it is not clear that particular behaviors, for instance indirect aggression, constitute bullying, these behaviors are more likely to be overlooked or minimized. In the study

in which we explored bullying from the perspectives of fourth and fifth grade students who self-identified as bullied and of their parents, teachers, and school administrators[4], the prevailing pattern that emerged was the difficulty the children and adults had in actually identifying bullying. All of the respondents considered bullying harmful, and their definitions demonstrated that they understood what constitutes bullying. Most adults and children referred to a power imbalance and intent to cause harm, and most included direct as well as indirect behaviors in their definitions. Few mentioned repetition, however, corresponding with the results of Siann and colleagues (1993. Still, analysis of the interviews revealed that the respondents did in fact incorporate repetition as they spoke about their views and responses to bullying[5] (Mishna, 2012, p. 104). Mishna, F. (2012). Bullying: A guide to research, intervention, and prevention. New York: Oxford University Press.

[52] Qualtrics: it is a private research software company stablished in Provo, Utah in 2002. Its software enables users to do many kinds of online data collection and analysis including (but not limited to) market research, customer satisfaction and loyalty, product and concept testing, employee evaluations and website feedback. See Scott, M. (2012, August 27). Customer research easier in digital era. USA Today. Retrieved from http://usatoday30.usatoday.com/MONEY/ usaedition/ 2012-08-28-Efficient-Small-Business-Ecommerce_CV_U.htm

[53] Seabees: These are members of the United States Naval Mobile Construction Battalion (CB). The word "Seabee" comes from the phonics of the initials "CB." See "Seabes:" History of the US Navy Seabees. (n.d.). Retrieved from http://www.seabeesmuseum.com/History.html

[54] Confidence Level: it refers to the percentage of all possible samples that can be expected to include the true population parameter. For example, suppose all possible samples were selected from the same population, and a confidence interval were computed for each sample. A 95% confidence level implies that 95% of the confidence intervals would include the true population parameter. See "Confidence Level:" Definition. (n.d.). Retrieved from http://stattrek.com/statistics/dictionary.aspx?definition=confidence_level

[55] Confidence Interval: A confidence interval gives an estimated range of values which is likely to include an unknown population parameter, the estimated range being calculated from a given set of sample data. If independent samples are taken repeatedly from the same population, and a confidence interval calculated for each sample, then a certain percentage

(confidence level) of the intervals will include the unknown population parameter. See "Confidence Interval:" Statistics Glossary (n.d.). Retrieved from http://www.stats.gla.ac.uk/steps /glossary/confidence_ intervals.html

[56] IRB: An institutional review board is a committee whose primary responsibility is to protect the rights and welfare of human research participants. Currently, no federal law or national directive requires all research to be reviewed in a uniform way regardless of researcher affiliation or funding source. In situations in which research is subject to federal regulation (e.g., involves the use of federal funds), the definition of an IRB and the procedures for research review are described in detail in the Code of Federal Regulations. When research is not subject to federal regulation, researchers are under no legal obligation to monitor the ethical aspects of research, but many elect to do so with a system modeled after the federal IRB system. See "IRB" (Bankert, Amdur, & Amdur, 2006, p. 24)

[57] Pay grade: Do not confuse rank with pay grades, such as E-1, W-2 and O-5. Pay grades are administrative classifications used primarily to standardize compensation across the military services. The "E" in E-1 stands for "enlisted" while the "1" indicates the pay grade for that position. The other pay categories are "W" for warrant officers and "O" for commissioned officers. Some enlisted pay grades have two ranks. See "Pay grade:" U.S. Navy Enlisted Rating Structure. (n.d.). Retrieved from http://bluejacket.com/usn_ratings.htm

[58] R: it is a free software programming language and software environment for statistical computing and graphics. "R" began as an experiment in trying to use the methods of Lisp implementers to build a small test-bed which could be used to trial some ideas on how a statistical environment might be built. Early on, the decision was made to use an S-like syntax. […] it has now outgrown its origins and its development is now a collaborative effort undertaken using the Internet to exchange ideas and distribute the results. See Ihaka, Ross (1998). R :Past and Future History. Interface98 (Technical report). Statistics Department, The University of Auckland, Auckland, New Zealand.

[59] Understanding Military Culture | Bama At Work. (n.d.). Retrieved from http://bamaatwork.com/2014/08/29/understanding-military-culture/

[60] Psychological reaction occurring after a highly stressful event and typically characterized by flashbacks, recurrent nightmares, and avoidance of reminders of the event; depression and anxiety are often present. Traumatic events that can lead to PTSD include automobile accidents, rape or assault, military

combat, torture, and such natural disasters as floods, fires, or earthquakes. Long-term effects can include marital and family problems, difficulties at work, and abuse of alcohol and other drugs. Antidepressant medication and psychotherapy, including group therapy, are used in treating the disorder. See "PTSD." (2009). Encyclopædia Britannica 2009 Ready Reference. Chicago: Encyclopædia Britannica.

[61] Mood swing: "are characterized by unexpected and sudden shifts in mood that are uncharacteristic of the person's usual mood. These may include outbursts of anger, almost out of the blue and out of all proportion to what's happening, aggressive behavior regarding inconsequential matters, and there may even be a sense of euphoria in which unrealistic plans are made or major changes in lifestyle are seen as viable" (Farrell, 2011, p. 11). Farrell, P. (2011). It's not all in your head: Anxiety, depression, mood swings, and multiple sclerosis. New York: Demos Health.

[62] Quandary: A situation or circumstance that presents problems difficult to solve :a state of perplexity or uncertainty, esp. as to what to do; dilemma :of uncertain origin; perhaps related to Latin quandō when]. Collins English Dictionary – Complete and Unabridged © HarperCollins Publishers 1991, 1994, 1998, 2000, 2003. See "quandary." (n.d.) The American Heritage® Dictionary of the English Language, Fourth Edition. (2003). Retrieved November 22, 2014
from http://www.thefreedictionary.com/quandaries

Appendix A

BUFFALO STATE
The State University of New York

- SITE AGREEMENT -

The undersign researcher is conducting a study project to determine how Supervisory Styles are related to workplace-stress in the US Navy Reserve. Work-related stress is already present in a large number of complaints in medical centers and hospitals across the nation. Among the common complaints, one can mention the increased blood pressure, depression, alcohol abuse and other psychosomatic disorders such as asthma, eczema, back pain, migraine, insomnia, and stomach ulcers.

The scope of this research study focuses attention on the perception of discomforts from supervisory and managerial policies and practices embracing supervisors and supervisees. The study encompasses any tension or pressure perceived by reservists, to the best of their recollection during their time spent in the US Navy Reserve. For this purpose, the researcher will be collecting data from a questionnaire containing 11 different multiple choice statements.

Your site participation is essential to this research project, and it is assured that it will be entirely voluntary. There is no risk involved with personal identifiers since all information is treated confidentially and used for this research purpose only. To maintain confidentiality, the consent and the questionnaire will be filed separately to guarantee sailors' anonymity, which ensure that participants cannot be identify individually. Moreover, sailors have the right to opt-out at any time as is stated in both documents (Consent From and Questionnaire).

Your consideration to this request is certainly appreciated. It will further the researcher graduate studies at SUNY Buffalo State, and it could benefit other scholars reviewing the subject matter of Supervision in Human Services. Furthermore, the researcher will be more than glad to share the results of the study once concluded if that is something you may be interested. Above all, feel free to contact me at 716-858-1830 with any further questions.

Miguel A. Reyes-Mariano
Political Science Department, MFA - Nonprofit Management

- __Y-6__ **I approve the study** described above and will move forward on approving the researcher to conduct it within my school

- ______ **I do not approve the study** described above and will not move forward on approving the researcher to conduct it within my school

Administrator Name: __ROBERT BONIPACE__ Facility Name: __NOSC BUFFALO__
(please print)

Administrator
Signature: _______________________ Date: __12 SEPT 14__

Note: If you are unable to reach the researcher and have general questions or you have concerns or complaints about the research study or questions about your rights as a research subject, please contact Gina Game, IRB Administrator, Sponsored Programs Office/SUNY Buffalo State at gamega@buffalostate.edu or (716) 878-6700.

Appendix B

BUFFALO STATE
The State University of New York

- SITE AGREEMENT -

The undersign researcher is conducting a study project to determine how Supervisory Styles are related to workplace-stress in the US Navy Reserve. Work-related stress is already present in a large number of complaints in medical centers and hospitals across the nation. Among the common complaints, one can mention the increased blood pressure, depression, alcohol abuse and other psychosomatic disorders such as asthma, eczema, back pain, migraine, insomnia, and stomach ulcers.

The scope of this research study focuses attention on the perception of discomforts from supervisory and managerial policies and practices embracing supervisors and supervisees. The study encompasses any tension or pressure perceived by reservists, to the best of their recollection during their time spent in the US Navy Reserve. For this purpose, the researcher will be collecting data from a questionnaire containing 31 different multiple choice statements.

Your site participation is essential to this research project, and it is assured that it will be entirely voluntary. There is no risk involved with personal identifiers since all information is treated confidentially and used for this research purpose only. To maintain confidentiality, the consent and the questionnaire will be filed separately to guarantee sailors' anonymity, which ensure that participants cannot be identify individually. Moreover, sailors have the right to opt-out at any time as is stated in both documents (Consent From and Questionnaire).

Your consideration to this request is certainly appreciated. It will further the researcher graduate studies at SUNY Buffalo State, and it could benefit other scholars reviewing the subject matter of Supervision in Human Services. Furthermore, the researcher will be more than glad to share the results of the study once concluded if that is something you may be interested. Above all, feel free to contact me at 716-858-1830 with any further questions.

Miguel A. Reyes-Mariano
Political Science Department, MPA - Nonprofit Management

- _✓_ **I approve the study** described above and will move forward on approving the researcher to conduct it within my school

- _____ **I do not approve the study** described above and will not move forward on approving the researcher to conduct it within my school

Administrator Name: _ENC RUDY MARIN_ Facility Name: _NOSC ROCHESTER_
(please print)

Administrator
Signature: _______________________ Date: _05 SEP 2014_

Note: If you are unable to reach the researcher and have general questions or you have concerns or complaints about the research study or questions about your rights as a research subject, please contact Gina Game, IRB Administrator, Sponsored Programs Office/SUNY Buffalo State at gameg@buffalostate.edu or (716) 878-6700.

Appendix C

BUFFALO STATE
The State University of New York

- SITE AGREEMENT -

The undersign researcher is conducting a study project to determine how Supervisory Styles are related to workplace-stress in the US Navy Reserve. Work-related stress is already present in a large number of complaints in medical centers and hospitals across the nation. Among the common complaints, one can mention the increased blood pressure, depression, alcohol abuse and other psychosomatic disorders such as asthma, eczema, back pain, migraine, insomnia, and stomach ulcers.

The scope of this research study focuses attention on the perception of discomforts from supervisory and managerial policies and practices embracing supervisors and supervisees. The study encompasses any tension or pressure perceived by reservists, to the best of their recollection during their time spent in the US Navy Reserve. For this purpose, the researcher will be collecting data from a questionnaire containing 31 different multiple choice statements.

Your site participation is essential to this research project, and it is assured that it will be entirely voluntary. There is no risk involved with personal identifiers since all information is treated confidentially and used for this research purpose only. To maintain confidentiality, the consent and the questionnaire will be filed separately to guarantee sailors' anonymity, which ensure that participants cannot be identify individually. Moreover, sailors have the right to opt-out at any time as is stated in both documents (Consent From and Questionnaire).

Your consideration to this request is certainly appreciated. It will further the researcher graduate studies at SUNY Buffalo State, and it could benefit other scholars reviewing the subject matter of Supervision in Human Services. Furthermore, the researcher will be more than glad to share the results of the study once concluded if that is something you may be interested. Above all, feel free to contact me at 716-858-1830 with any further questions.

Miguel A. Reyes-Mariano
Political Science Department, MPA - Nonprofit Management

- _____✓_____ **I approve the study** described above and will move forward on approving the researcher to conduct it within my school

- __________ **I do not approve the study** described above and will not move forward on approving the researcher to conduct it within my school

Administrator Name: _Shawn Reynolds_   Facility Name: _NOSC Syracuse_
(please print)

Administrator
Signature: _Shawn Boel_   Date: _9/6/14_

Note: If you are unable to reach the researcher and have general questions or you have concerns or complaints about the research study or questions about your rights as a research subject, please contact Gina Game, IRB Administrator, Sponsored Programs Office/SUNY Buffalo State at gameg@buffalostate.edu or (716) 878-6700.

Appendix D

BUFFALO STATE
The State University of New York

- INFORMED CONSENT -

STRESS' IMPACT OF SUPERVISORY STYLES IN US NAVY RESERVISTS

RESEARCHER: Miguel A. Reyes-Mariano, Master in Public Administration – Political Science Department at SUNY Buffalo State. Classrooms A-301 * 716-858-1830 * reyesmma01@mail.buffalostate.edu

STUDY LOCATIONS: NOSC Buffalo, Rochester and Syracuse in the State of New York.

PURPOSE OF STUDY: The purpose of this study is to explore how supervisory styles relate to stress on US Navy reservists drilling in Naval Operational Support Centers Buffalo, Rochester and Syracuse in the state of New York.

INCLUSION REQUIREMENTS: Members of US Navy Reserve drilling in established study locations.

PROCEDURES: As a survey research, this study involves the collection of information through a questionnaire. The questionnaire will be administered through your unit CO and then returned to the NOSC's Chief. To maintain confidentiality, this consent, and the questionnaire will be filed separately to ensure your anonymity.

RISKS: The potential risk of this study is very minimal, since the confidentiality measures have been guaranteed.

BENEFITS: The result could show with statistical significance if supervisory styles in place are related to workplace stress, and corrective actions could be taken to benefit the operational conditions of US Navy reservists.

CONFIDENTIALITY: Your participation is essential to this research project, and it is assured that it will be entirely voluntary. There is no risk involved with personal identifiers since all information is treated confidentially and used for this research purpose only. To maintain confidentiality, the consent and the questionnaire will be filed separately to guarantee your anonymity, which also ensure that participants cannot be identify individually. Moreover, you have the right to opt-out at any time as is stated in the questionnaire.

QUESTIONS: For any comments, concerns, or inquiries regarding this research, please contact the researcher at the top of this form. If you are unable to contact the researcher and have questions about your rights as a participant, contact Gina Game, IRB Administrator, Sponsored Programs Office/State University of New York - Buffalo State at gameg@buffalostate.edu

VOLUNTARY PARTICIPATION STATEMENT: Participation in this study is voluntary. You may refuse to answer any question or opt out at any time. (Your decision will not affect your future relationship with SUNY Buffalo State). If you have any questions about this research study, please ask to your chain of command or contact the researcher before you complete the questionnaire. Your signature below indicates that you have read the information in this informed consent and you have had a chance to ask any questions that you may have about the study.

SIGNATURES

____   _______________
Participant's Signature   Date

____   _______________
Researcher's Signature   Date

Appendix E (p. 1)

STRESS IN THE U.S. MILITARY RESERVE

STRESS' IMPACT OF SUPERVISORY STYLES - QUESTIONNAIRE

Your responses are voluntary and will be confidential. Responses will not be identified by individual.
All responses will be compiled together and analyzed as a group. Please do not write your name.

By completing this questionnaire you are consenting to participate in this research
— You can opt out of this survey at any time —

*** PLEASE MARK THE APPROPRIATE RESPONSE ***

AGE IN YEARS	○ 18-20, ○ 21-25, ○ 26-30, ○ 31-35, ○ 36-40, ○ 41-45, ○ 46-50, ○ 51-60 years
SEX	○ Male, ○ Female
ETHNICITY	○ White, ○ African descent, ○ Latino, ○ Asian, ○ Native American, ○ Pacific, ○ Mixed Race
TIME IN SERVICE	○ Less than 1 year, ○ 1-5, ○ 6-10, ○ 11-15, ○ 16-20, ○ 21+ years
PAY GRADE	○ E-1, ○ E2, ○ E3, ○ E4, ○ E5, ○ E6, ○ E7, ○ E8, ○ E9
	○ WO1, ○ WO2, ○ WO3, ○ O1, ○ O2, ○ O3, ○ O4, ○ O5, ○ O6, ○ O7
TIME IN GRADE	○ Less than 1 year, ○ 1-4, ○ 5-8, ○ 9-12, ○ 13-16, ○ 17-20, ○ 21+ years
EDUCATION	○ A School-Technical, ○ Associate's, ○ Mil. Academy-Bachelor's, ○ Master's, ○ PhD

	0 Times	1 - 2 Times	3 - 4 Times	5 + Times	Every drill-day
01) How frequently do you experience a mood change after leaving the workplace?	○	○	○	○	○
02) In a typical work day, how often do you feel stressed?	○	○	○	○	○
03) How often your supervisor gives you feedback about your work in a typical work day?	○	○	○	○	○
04) How often you felt harassed by your supervisor this year?	○	○	○	○	○
05) How often you felt bullied by your supervisor this year?	○	○	○	○	○
06) How often you felt discriminated by your supervisor this year?	○	○	○	○	○

	Not Satisfied	Moderately Satisfied	Satisfied	Very Satisfied	N/A
07) How satisfied are you with the autonomy your supervisor gives you to complete your work?	○	○	○	○	○
08) How satisfied are you with the work of those reporting to you?	○	○	○	○	○

	Very Well	Well	Moderately Well	Not Well at all
09) How well are responsibilities shared among your team members?	○	○	○	○
10) How well do you know your Command's mission?	○	○	○	○
11) How well do you know your Command's structure?	○	○	○	○
12) How well do you know your Command's operations?	○	○	○	○
13) How well you and your supervisor communicate with each other?	○	○	○	○

*** PLEASE SEE REVERSE ***

Appendix E (p. 2)

	Strongly-Agree	Agree	Disagree	Strongly-Disagree
14) When at work, I feel defensive towards my supervisor.	○	○	○	○
15) My supervisor has always been involved in my career development planning.	○	○	○	○
16) My supervisor clearly explained the Command's mission at my arrival.	○	○	○	○
17) My supervisor clearly explained the Command's structure at my arrival.	○	○	○	○
18) My supervisor clearly explained the Command's operations at my arrival.	○	○	○	○
19) I know exactly what is expected from me at all times.	○	○	○	○
20) I have access to the necessary resources to carry out my work.	○	○	○	○
21) My supervisor and I have a good working relationship.	○	○	○	○
22) My Command is constantly contributing to my professional development.	○	○	○	○
23) When at work, stress reduces the quality of my performance.	○	○	○	○
24) After leaving the military-workplace, I need alcohol to reduce my stress.	○	○	○	○
25) Before or after a drill-day I experience sleep problems.	○	○	○	○

	Not Easy at all	Moderately Easy	Very Easy	Extremely Easy
26) How easy is to find opportunities will help advance your military career at your work center?	○	○	○	○

	Strongly-Agree	Agree	Disagree	Strongly-Disagree
27) The example of my Supervisor is very inspiring to meet my goals at work	○	○	○	○
28) The work pace expected from you at your workplace is always reasonable	○	○	○	○
29) I frequently experience unexplained anger after leaving the workplace.	○	○	○	○
30) I feel there is no other place I perfectly fit in outside my military life.	○	○	○	○
31) I am excited about the meaningfulness of my work.	○	○	○	○

If you would like to add any comments that you consider appropriate, please feel free to do so in the space below:

____

____

____

____

____

Thank you for taking the time to participate in this survey; your information is very valuable.

– You can opt out of this survey at any time –

Appendix F

Required Sample Size[†]

Population Size	Confidence = 95% Margin of Error				Confidence = 99% Margin of Error			
	5.0%	3.5%	2.5%	1.0%	5.0%	3.5%	2.5%	1.0%
10	10	10	10	10	10	10	10	10
20	19	20	20	20	19	20	20	20
30	28	29	29	30	29	29	30	30
50	44	47	48	50	47	48	49	50
75	63	69	72	74	67	71	73	75
100	80	89	94	99	87	93	96	99

Figures and Tables

FIGURES

Figure #1: Reserve Components as of November 26th 2014

Reserve Components
NOBLE EAGLE / ENDURING FREEDOM

Unique SSAN Activations as of: November 25, 2014

		Change from last week
Currently Activated:	**30,050**	(-98)
Deactivated Since 9/11:	**872,755**	
Total:	**902,805**	

Reserve Component	* Current Involuntary Activations	Change from last week	** Current Voluntary Activations	Change from last week	Total Currently Activated	Change from last week	***Total Deactivated Since 9/11	***Total Activated Since 9/11
ARNG	7,993	(-86)	806	(-4)	8,799	(-90)	373,698	382,497
USAR	8,951	(-62)	1,032	(+9)	9,983	(-53)	210,942	220,925
USNR	2,830	(-29)	201	(+3)	3,031	(-26)	52,923	55,954
USMCR	334	(+1)	643	(+6)	977	(+7)	62,059	63,036
ANG	1,958	(+133)	2,285	(-138)	4,243	(-5)	98,594	102,837
USAFR	1,140	(+53)	1,577	(+16)	2,717	(+69)	66,337	69,054
USCGR	149	(+0)	151	(+2)	300	(+2)	8,202	8,502
TOTAL	23,355	(+8)	6,695	(-106)	30,050	(-98)	872,755	902,805

Notes:
* Includes members placed on Active Duty under 10 USC Sections 688, 12301(a), 12302 and 12304
** Includes members placed on Active Duty under 10 USC 12301(d) and members categorized as unknown in CTS statute code
***Includes members who were activated for OPERATION IRAQI FREEDOM / OPERATION NEW DAWN
DRS# 21600
Source: Contingency Tracking System (CTS) Daily Processing Files

Produced by the Defense Manpower Data Center

a.

Figure #2: Email form Professor Lawrence Shulman, consenting permission to adapt questionnaires form his textbook "International Supervision" (3rd Edition).

STRESS IN THE U.S. MILITARY RESERVE

TABLES

Final Report
Last Modified: 09/16/2014

1. Age in years

#	Answer		Response	%
1	18-20		2	3.64%
2	21-25		7	12.73%
3	26-30		15	27.27%
4	31-35		13	23.64%
5	36-40		6	10.91%
6	41-45		3	5.45%
7	46-50		7	12.73%
8	51-60		2	3.64%
	Total		55	100.00%

Statistic		Value
Min Value		1
Max Value		8
Mean		4.11
Variance		3.21
Standard Deviation		1.79
Total Responses		55

2. Sex

#	Answer		Response	%
1	Male		43	79.63%
2	Female		11	20.37%
	Total		54	100.00%

Statistic	Value
Min Value	1
Max Value	2
Mean	1.20
Variance	0.17
Standard Deviation	0.41
Total Responses	54

3. Ethnicity

#	Answer		Response	%
1	White		49	89.09%
2	African descent		1	1.82%
3	Latino		2	3.64%
4	Asian		0	0.00%
5	Native American		1	1.82%
6	Pacific		1	1.82%
7	Mixed Race		1	1.82%
	Total		55	100.00%

Statistic	Value
Min Value	1
Max Value	7
Mean	1.36
Variance	1.46
Standard Deviation	1.21
Total Responses	55

4. Time in service

#	Answer		Response	%
1	Less than 1 year		2	3.64%
2	1-5 years		11	20.00%
3	6-10 years		17	30.91%
4	11-15 years		13	23.64%
5	16-20 years		10	18.18%
6	21+ years		2	3.64%
	Total		55	100.00%

STRESS IN THE U.S. MILITARY RESERVE

Statistic	Value
Min Value	1
Max Value	6
Mean	3.44
Variance	1.47
Standard Deviation	1.21
Total Responses	55

5. Pay grade -E

#	Answer		Response	%
1	E-1		0	0.00%
2	E-2		1	1.92%
3	E-3		4	7.69%
4	E-4		9	17.31%
5	E-5		18	34.62%
6	E-6		15	28.85%
7	E-7		5	9.62%
8	E-8		0	0.00%
9	E-9		0	0.00%
	Total		52	100.00%

Statistic	Value
Min Value	2
Max Value	7
Mean	5.10
Variance	1.34
Standard Deviation	1.16
Total Responses	52

6. Pay grade -O

#	Answer		Response	%
1	WO-1		0	0.00%
2	WO-2		0	0.00%
3	WO-3		1	25.00%
4	O-1		0	0.00%
5	O-2		1	25.00%
6	O-3		1	25.00%
7	O-4		1	25.00%
8	O-5		0	0.00%
9	O-6		0	0.00%
10	O-7		0	0.00%
	Total		4	100.00%

Statistic	Value
Min Value	3
Max Value	7
Mean	5.25
Variance	2.92
Standard Deviation	1.71
Total Responses	4

7. Time in grade

#	Answer		Response	%
1	Less than 1 year		6	10.71%
2	1-4 years		30	53.57%
3	5-8 years		14	25.00%
4	9-12 years		3	5.36%
5	13-16 years		1	1.79%
6	17-20 years		2	3.57%
7	21+ years		0	0.00%
	Total		56	100.00%

Statistic	Value
Min Value	1
Max Value	6
Mean	2.45
Variance	1.12
Standard Deviation	1.06
Total Responses	56

8. Education

#	Answer		Response	%
1	A-School / Technical		18	36.73%
2	Associate's		12	24.49%
3	Mil.Academy / Bachelor's		15	30.61%
4	Master's		4	8.16%
5	PhD		0	0.00%
	Total		49	100.00%

Statistic		Value
Min Value		1
Max Value		4
Mean		2.10
Variance		1.01
Standard Deviation		1.01
Total Responses		49

9. Q.01- How frequently do you experience a mood change after leaving the workplace? (past year)

#	Answer		Response	%
1	0 Times		16	27.59%
2	1-2 Times		17	29.31%
3	3-4 Times		12	20.69%
4	5+ Times		1	1.72%
5	Every Drill day		12	20.69%
	Total		58	100.00%

Statistic		Value
Min Value		1
Max Value		5
Mean		2.59
Variance		2.11
Standard Deviation		1.45
Total Responses		58

10. Q.02- In a typical workday, how often do you feel stressed?

#	Answer		Response	%
1	0 Times		11	18.97%
2	1-2 Times		30	51.72%
3	3-4 Times		13	22.41%
4	5+ Times		0	0.00%
5	Every drill day		4	6.90%
	Total		58	100.00%

Statistic		Value
Min Value		1
Max Value		5
Mean		2.24
Variance		0.99
Standard Deviation		1.00
Total Responses		58

11. Q.03- How often your supervisor gives you feedback about your work in a typical workday?

#	Answer	Response	%
1	0 Times	20	34.48%
2	1-2 Times	26	44.83%
3	3-4 Times	7	12.07%
4	5+ Times	1	1.72%
5	Every drill day	4	6.90%
	Total	58	100.00%

Statistic		Value
Min Value		1
Max Value		5
Mean		2.02
Variance		1.18
Standard Deviation		1.08
Total Responses		58

12. Q.04- How often you felt harassed by your supervisor this year?

#	Answer	Response	%
1	0 Times	45	77.59%
2	1-2 Times	9	15.52%
3	3-4 Times	1	1.72%
4	5+ Times	2	3.45%
5	Every drill day	1	1.72%
	Total	58	100.00%

Statistic		Value
Min Value		1
Max Value		5
Mean		1.36
Variance		0.69
Standard Deviation		0.83
Total Responses		58

13. Q.05- How often you felt bullied by your supervisor this year?

#	Answer		Response	%
1	0 Times		48	82.76%
2	1-2 Times		5	8.62%
3	3-4 Times		2	3.45%
4	5+ Times		1	1.72%
5	Every drill day		2	3.45%
	Total		58	100.00%

Statistic		Value
Min Value		1
Max Value		5
Mean		1.34
Variance		0.83
Standard Deviation		0.91
Total Responses		58

14. Q.06- How often you felt discriminated by your supervisor this year?

#	Answer		Response	%
1	0 Times		52	89.66%
2	1-2 Times		2	3.45%
3	3-4 Times		2	3.45%
4	5+ Times		1	1.72%
5	Every drill day		1	1.72%
	Total		58	100.00%

Statistic	Value
Min Value	1
Max Value	5
Mean	1.22
Variance	0.56
Standard Deviation	0.75
Total Responses	58

15. Q.07- How satisfied are you with the autonomy your supervisor gives you to complete your work?

#	Answer		Response	%
1	Not Satisfied		2	3.45%
2	Moderately Satisfied		10	17.24%
3	Satisfied		27	46.55%
4	Very Satisfied		17	29.31%
5	N/A		2	3.45%
	Total		58	100.00%

Statistic	Value
Min Value	1
Max Value	5
Mean	3.12
Variance	0.74
Standard Deviation	0.86
Total Responses	58

16. Q.08- How satisfied are you with the work of those reporting to you?

#	Answer		Response	%
1	Not Satisfied		1	1.72%
2	Moderately Satisfied		6	10.34%
3	Satisfied		25	43.10%
4	Very Satisfied		11	18.97%
5	N/A		15	25.86%
	Total		58	100.00%

Statistic		Value
Min Value		1
Max Value		5
Mean		3.57
Variance		1.09
Standard Deviation		1.04
Total Responses		58

17. Q.09- How well are responsibilities shared among your team members?

#	Answer		Response	%
1	Very Well		7	12.07%
2	Well		19	32.76%
3	Moderately Well		22	37.93%
4	Not well at all		10	17.24%
	Total		58	100.00%

Statistic		Value
Min Value		1
Max Value		4
Mean		2.60
Variance		0.84
Standard Deviation		0.92
Total Responses		58

18. Q.10- How well do you know your Command's mission?

#	Answer		Response	%
1	Very Well		17	29.31%
2	Well		18	31.03%
3	Moderately Well		17	29.31%
4	Not well at all		6	10.34%
	Total		58	100.00%

Statistic		Value
Min Value		1
Max Value		4
Mean		2.21
Variance		0.97
Standard Deviation		0.99
Total Responses		58

19. Q.11- How well do you know your Command's structure?

#	Answer		Response	%
1	Very Well		19	32.76%
2	Well		21	36.21%
3	Moderately Well		14	24.14%
4	Not well at all		4	6.90%
	Total		58	100.00%

Statistic	Value
Min Value	1
Max Value	4
Mean	2.05
Variance	0.86
Standard Deviation	0.93
Total Responses	58

20. Q.12- How well do you know your Command's operations?

#	Answer		Response	%
1	Very Well		18	31.03%
2	Well		17	29.31%
3	Moderately Well		15	25.86%
4	Not well at all		8	13.79%
	Total		58	100.00%

Statistic	Value
Min Value	1
Max Value	4
Mean	2.22
Variance	1.09
Standard Deviation	1.04
Total Responses	58

21. Q.13- How well you and your supervisor communicate with each other?

#	Answer		Response	%
1	Very Well		20	34.48%
2	Well		16	27.59%
3	Moderately Well		14	24.14%
4	Not well at all		8	13.79%
	Total		58	100.00%

Statistic	Value
Min Value	1
Max Value	4
Mean	2.17
Variance	1.13
Standard Deviation	1.06
Total Responses	58

22. Q.14- When at work, I feel defensive towards my supervisor.

#	Answer		Response	%
1	Strongly-agree		2	3.57%
2	Agree		7	12.50%
3	Disagree		27	48.21%
4	Strongly-disagree		20	35.71%
	Total		56	100.00%

Statistic	Value
Min Value	1
Max Value	4
Mean	3.16
Variance	0.61
Standard Deviation	0.78
Total Responses	56

23. Q.15- My supervisor has always been involved in my career development planning.

#	Answer		Response	%
1	Strongly-agree		8	14.29%
2	Agree		29	51.79%
3	Disagree		16	28.57%
4	Strongly-disagree		3	5.36%
	Total		56	100.00%

Statistic	Value
Min Value	1
Max Value	4
Mean	2.25
Variance	0.59
Standard Deviation	0.77
Total Responses	56

24. Q.16- My supervisor clearly explained the Command's mission at my arrival.

#	Answer		Response	%
1	Strongly-agree		9	16.07%
2	Agree		28	50.00%
3	Disagree		12	21.43%
4	Strongly-disagree		7	12.50%
	Total		56	100.00%

Statistic	Value
Min Value	1
Max Value	4
Mean	2.30
Variance	0.80
Standard Deviation	0.89
Total Responses	56

25. Q.17- My supervisor clearly explained the Command's structure at my arrival.

#	Answer		Response	%
1	Strongly-agree		8	14.29%
2	Agree		28	50.00%
3	Disagree		16	28.57%
4	Strongly-disagree		4	7.14%
	Total		56	100.00%

Statistic	Value
Min Value	1
Max Value	4
Mean	2.29
Variance	0.64
Standard Deviation	0.80
Total Responses	56

26. Q.18- My supervisor clearly explained the Command's operations at my arrival.

#	Answer		Response	%
1	Strongly-agree		8	14.29%
2	Agree		27	48.21%
3	Disagree		16	28.57%
4	Strongly-disagree		5	8.93%
	Total		56	100.00%

Statistic	Value
Min Value	1
Max Value	4
Mean	2.32
Variance	0.69
Standard Deviation	0.83
Total Responses	56

27. Q.19- I know exactly what is expected from me at all times.-

#	Answer		Response	%
1	Strongly-agree		14	25.00%
2	Agree		28	50.00%
3	Disagree		9	16.07%
4	Strongly-disagree		5	8.93%
	Total		56	100.00%

Statistic	Value
Min Value	1
Max Value	4
Mean	2.09
Variance	0.77
Standard Deviation	0.88
Total Responses	56

28. Q.20- I have access to the necessary resources to carry out my work.

#	Answer		Response	%
1	Strongly-agree		7	12.50%
2	Agree		29	51.79%
3	Disagree		16	28.57%
4	Strongly-disagree		4	7.14%
	Total		56	100.00%

Statistic	Value
Min Value	1
Max Value	4
Mean	2.30
Variance	0.62
Standard Deviation	0.78
Total Responses	56

29. Q.21- My supervisor and I have a good working relationship.

#	Answer		Response	%
1	Strongly-agree		19	33.93%
2	Agree		26	46.43%
3	Disagree		9	16.07%
4	Strongly-disagree		2	3.57%
	Total		56	100.00%

Statistic	Value
Min Value	1
Max Value	4
Mean	1.89
Variance	0.64
Standard Deviation	0.80
Total Responses	56

30. Q.22- My Command is constantly contributing to my professional development.

#	Answer		Response	%
1	Strongly-agree		9	16.07%
2	Agree		27	48.21%
3	Disagree		15	26.79%
4	Strongly-disagree		5	8.93%
	Total		56	100.00%

Statistic	Value
Min Value	1
Max Value	4
Mean	2.29
Variance	0.72
Standard Deviation	0.85
Total Responses	56

31. Q.23- When at work, stress reduces the quality of my performance.

#	Answer		Response	%
1	Strongly-agree		5	8.93%
2	Agree		15	26.79%
3	Disagree		23	41.07%
4	Strongly-disagree		13	23.21%
	Total		56	100.00%

Statistic	Value
Min Value	1
Max Value	4
Mean	2.79
Variance	0.83
Standard Deviation	0.91
Total Responses	56

32. Q.24- After leaving the military-workplace, I need alcohol to reduce my stress.

#	Answer		Response	%
1	Strongly-agree		3	5.36%
2	Agree		6	10.71%
3	Disagree		19	33.93%
4	Strongly-disagree		28	50.00%
	Total		56	100.00%

Statistic	Value
Min Value	1
Max Value	4
Mean	3.29
Variance	0.75
Standard Deviation	0.87
Total Responses	56

33. Q.25- Before or after a drill-day I experience sleep problems.

#	Answer		Response	%
1	Strongly-agree		4	7.14%
2	Agree		9	16.07%
3	Disagree		21	37.50%
4	Strongly-disagree		22	39.29%
	Total		56	100.00%

Statistic	Value
Min Value	1
Max Value	4
Mean	3.09
Variance	0.85
Standard Deviation	0.92
Total Responses	56

34. Q.26- How easy is to find opportunities will help advance your military career at your work center?

#	Answer		Response	%
1	Not easy at all		21	37.50%
2	Moderately easy		24	42.86%
3	Very easy		8	14.29%
4	Extremely easy		3	5.36%
	Total		56	100.00%

Statistic	Value
Min Value	1
Max Value	4
Mean	1.88
Variance	0.73
Standard Deviation	0.85
Total Responses	56

35. Q.27- The example of my Supervisor is very inspiring to meet my goals at work

#	Answer		Response	%
1	Strongly-agree		6	10.71%
2	Agree		33	58.93%
3	Disagree		11	19.64%
4	Strongly-disagree		6	10.71%
	Total		56	100.00%

Statistic	Value
Min Value	1
Max Value	4
Mean	2.30
Variance	0.65
Standard Deviation	0.81
Total Responses	56

36. Q.28- The work pace expected from you at your workplace is always reasonable

#	Answer		Response	%
1	Strongly-agree		8	14.29%
2	Agree		34	60.71%
3	Disagree		11	19.64%
4	Strongly-disagree		3	5.36%
	Total		56	100.00%

Statistic	Value
Min Value	1
Max Value	4
Mean	2.16
Variance	0.54
Standard Deviation	0.73
Total Responses	56

37. Q.29- I frequently experience unexplained anger after leaving the workplace.

#	Answer		Response	%
1	Strongly-agree		3	5.36%
2	Agree		5	8.93%
3	Disagree		27	48.21%
4	Strongly-disagree		21	37.50%
	Total		56	100.00%

Statistic	Value
Min Value	1
Max Value	4
Mean	3.18
Variance	0.66
Standard Deviation	0.81
Total Responses	56

38. Q.30- I feel there is no other place I perfectly fit in outside my military life.

#	Answer		Response	%
1	Strongly-agree		5	8.93%
2	Agree		1	1.79%
3	Disagree		21	37.50%
4	Strongly-disagree		29	51.79%
	Total		56	100.00%

Statistic	Value
Min Value	1
Max Value	4
Mean	3.32
Variance	0.80
Standard Deviation	0.90
Total Responses	56

39. Q.31- I am excited about the meaningfulness of my work.

#	Answer		Response	%
1	Strongly-agree		15	26.79%
2	Agree		29	51.79%
3	Disagree		9	16.07%
4	Strongly-disagree		3	5.36%
	Total		56	100.00%

Statistic	Value
Min Value	1
Max Value	4
Mean	2.00
Variance	0.65
Standard Deviation	0.81
Total Responses	56

40. Comments

#	Answer		Response	%
1	Click to write Choice 1		7	100.00%
	Total		7	100.00%

Comments.../

Q.#1 -I have experienced positive mood changes.

Q.#2 -I felt stressed due to the lack of hands-on training, not related to supervision.

-I find my command has enabled my success so far and loves the navy.

Comments from e-mails sent directly to researcher:

-Being in trailers is not helping with the communications. I think Navy Reservists need a lot more mentoring, and every sailor should have an E-5 or E-6 as a mentor.

-There is an ongoing problem of lack of communication.

-People are finding it hard to advance, and the burden comes from not having particular unit's duties, which leads to poor evaluations, which leads to decreased chance to advance.

-The lack of shared responsibilities is a critical issue because people do not feel their supervisors care when they are not given any responsibilities to them. However, there are only so many unit specific tasks that can be dealt out. I do believe this is a great source of frustration.

Statistic	Value
Min Value	1
Max Value	1
Mean	1.00
Variance	0.00
Standard Deviation	0.00
Total Responses	3